Why Hillary?

WHY HILLARY?

Wije Charles

ISBN – 13: 978-1537138107

ISBN – 10: 1537138103

Cover photo: *Situation Room*

The photograph was taken on May 1, 2011 at 4.06pm by White House photographer Pete Souza in the White House Situation Room.

The photographer captured this iconic image of President Obama, Vice President Joe Biden, Brig. Gen. Marshall B. Brad Webb, Defense Secretary Robert Gates, Secretary of State Hillary Clinton, and other heavy-hitters watching the raid on Osama bin Laden's compound in Pakistan.

Two dozen Special Forces operatives entered bin Laden's hidden compound during the night, and after a firefight killed the most wanted terrorist in modern times and took custody of his body.

The President and his national security team were receiving a live video feed provided by drones hovering above bin Laden's compound.

To my Little Kitty

You came to me on your own and lived with me for a few short years, always my friend and my only friend most of the time.

Political pundits, TV News casters, Talk Radio hosts, and most politicians claim that the electorate is angry with the Establishment.

This is not quite true.

The Democratic half of the electorate is not angry at all with their president, his administration or their party. They are just frustrated with the Republicans who allowed the Tea Partiers to make them "the party of No"

I'll tell you who is angry.

The Tea Partiers and the Establishment Republicans are mad as hell with each other.

Tea Partiers are mad because Obama is still in the White House and the Establishment Republicans didn't do anything about it. They believe they have been used and let down.

The Establishment Republicans are mad because the Tea Partiers prevented them from governing and their voters have had enough. They should have known better.

CONTENTS

Prologue

Chapters

PROLOGUE

If Trump becomes president

As the nominee of the Republican Party, Mr. Trump has a real possibility of becoming the next president of the United States.

Following is what I predict would happen if that possibility were to become real.

Trump's closest friends and worst enemies would agree unanimously that Trump sincerely believes that he is always right on any subject. We have seen and heard this throughout his campaign. He has said that he listens to himself. Indeed it earned him admiration and respect among his supporters.

This attitude of his would be reinforced ten-fold if he were to win the election and becomes president. He will believe that what he has campaigned on is what is best for the country and who can find fault with him for that? He will set about implementing what he promised. Any advice by Republican elders or his close friends to take it easy or go slow will be treated by Trump with contempt.

When you are the president of the United States, you live in a different world. There will be enough and more power hungry 'yes men' he can surround himself with.

Some Americans will be carried away with the aura of a beautiful white family back in the white house. Tea Partiers will be exuberant. Most Americans will wish him well which is the way it should be.

And then he will start implementing the agenda he campaigned on.

I believe the first will be the building of his beautiful wall on the southern border. That's a promise he never wavered on. If Trump wins he is sure to have a Republican House of Representatives and Senate. They wouldn't dare deny him necessary approvals. Fox News and Talk Radio will take care of any Republican defectors.

Construction of his beautiful wall will necessarily lead to problems with our southern neighbor. The Mexican government will not only refuse to contribute financially towards the wall, they will also not cooperate in any manner with its construction. Trump will start messing with NAFTA and will also want to impose all sorts of taxes and tariffs on Mexico and Mexicans living in the U.S.

It wouldn't be long before our trade relations with the other NAFTA partner and our northern neighbor Canada will start to deteriorate.

I have no idea what this would lead to except that it would be something bad. A trade war with our neighbors is a distinct possibility and wouldn't help the economy.

If not simultaneously with the construction of the wall, certainly not too long thereafter, Trump will start deporting 11 million undocumented immigrants, another main campaign promise. Again, a Republican House and a Republican Senate will not dare not to find him funds and pass the necessary legislation. That's when I believe a little bit of hell will break loose in some states. We have seen what has already happened outside Trump's rallies during his campaign. The Police and other security forces will sooner or later get it under control. I would say sooner because Trump will let them loose with no restrains. Trump would still have the support of most Republicans. After all, this is what they have been quietly hoping for quite some time. Fox News and talk Radio will be in their elements.

This is when the whispers will start around the world questioning "what's going on in America?" "Isn't this how it started in Nazi Germany?" The world wouldn't have seen anything like this since the Second World War except in places like Uganda under Idi Amin.

I don't think world opinion will bother Trump in the least. Trump will go ahead with another of his campaign promises: to institute a temporary ban on Muslims entering United States. Paul Ryan, if he is still the speaker of the house will not say "boo" to Trump. Ryan, for all his talk is just another weak, self centered politician.

What will happen when the Muslim ban is in place? I can only make a few guesses and hope that I am wrong.

Inside the U.S. it will be harder for our police, FBI and Home Land Security to trace the so called "lone wolves." Muslim communities that are already nervous will start to live in fear. Attacks against Muslims that are random now will become common place. Muslims will shut themselves off. That unfortunately is the natural reaction.

Terrorists everywhere in the world will use the Muslim ban as a recruitment tool for their murderous acts. It will help to spread their false narrative that Americans are the enemy of Muslims.

I do not know what will happen to relationships between American and Muslim armies that jointly fight terrorism in other countries. I cannot even guess.

All I know is that it will be a scary time.

That said, the United States is the strongest country in the world. We would overcome not one but many of the likes of Trump. The smart thing though is to avoid catastrophe.

It is time to take a good look at the upcoming election which is only three months away.

Presidential Election 2016

We are in 2016, another presidential election year and politicians, political pundits and newscasters all claim that this is the most consequential election of all time.

If this election is that consequential, why did one major political party, the Republicans, elect the businessman from New York Donald J. Trump as its nominee? It is not my place to suggest that he is unworthy of the GOP nomination, but it's the

Republican leaders that have been saying so from the day he announced his candidacy. It is no secret that the Establishment Republicans were desperate to stop Trump from getting the nomination. Well, they failed and Trump is their nominee and effectively the leader of their Party.

Democrats have Secretary Hillary Clinton as their nominee. Independent Senator Bernie Sanders from Vermont gave Hillary a run for her money for the Democratic Party nomination, just as she did to then Senator Obama in the 2008 campaign. When it was all over, Hillary backed Obama unconditionally. Bernie had to be dragged in.

My take is, not that this election is the most consequential; it's just that every presidential election is equally consequential. Voters have to be careful whom they elect as their president in every election. When they don't, they pay a price - like the collapse of the economy, the financial sector and the Housing industry in 2007/2008. You can top it up with two unnecessary wars.

I have lived under different administrations for quite some time. I know the difference they made on my middle class family. I felt it right that I openly express my concerns about the upcoming election. I have heard somewhere that "bad things happen when good people remain silent." Don't grudge me considering myself to be 'good.' Trumpster says he is the 'best.'

My views are based mostly on the campaign that Mr. Trump is running and the presidencies of George H.W. Bush, Bill Clinton, George W. Bush and the current president Barack Obama.

The prevailing conditions in the Democratic and Republican parties and the actions of their congressional representatives did play a major role in consolidating my views.

America is blessed with a form of government in which three co-equal branches, the executive, the legislature and the judiciary are responsible for the governance of the nation.

Unfortunately, when Barack Obama became president, the congressional Republicans made a calculated decision to abandon their responsibility to govern. Instead, they decided to totally obstruct the president's agenda. They actually boast that they are the 'party of No.'

Another reason that encouraged me to write this book is the degree to which the media has gleefully contributed to politics of personal destruction.

I am not referring to gossip tabloids. We need them for a little harmless fun and nobody really takes them seriously.

Talk radio has gone so far down the gutter that it's hard to listen. Most talk radio hosts are diehard supporters of the Tea Party. It got really nasty and vulgar after Obama was elected president. The filthy venom they spew twenty four – seven is partly responsible for the state that the Republican Party finds itself in today. They embraced the Tea Party, made use of them and are reaping what they sowed.

Social media can do serious damage to political parties and politicians, but my experience is that the damage is short-lived – explosive today and diffused by tomorrow.

Fox News Channel with their claim to 'fair and balanced' reporting is really the Republican Party's propaganda machine. To their credit, most of its hosts don't even bother to pretend otherwise.

My real beef is with the rest of the media.

Real damage to the political process is done when major newspapers and TV channels publish and promote stories purely for their sensationalism. In investigative journalism the reporter has to go where the story takes him or her without favor or prejudice. That is fine and the way as it should be, but unfortunately it is not what happens some of the time. Not all reporters, but some, slant or omit facts in their reporting in ever so subtle manner that it would distort the story. Done repetitively, this could destroy or build up a person. This makes it worse for politicians because those in the opposing party are ever ready to run away with any damaging story irrespective of its truthfulness.

Even her political opponents will admit that all media have been unfair to Secretary Clinton over almost a quarter of a century. That is an understatement, most of the time they have been downright hostile to her.

The opposite was the case with Mr. Donald Trump during the primaries. From the day he announced his candidacy, media build him up by providing him with free and unlimited news coverage.

It matters less that most reporters may have done it for pure sensationalism and ratings. Bottom line, they have, maybe unwittingly, assisted him to virtually destroy his primary opponents. The material Trump used to bring down his fellow candidates was nothing but ugly insults. Media published them for him for free.

We can only hope that media will treat both Hillary Clinton and Donald Trump on a more even keel as we head to the general election.

So, you have my book before you. I hope it's not yet November 7th 2016. If however, the election has already been held and we have a president-elect or a new president, do continue reading anyway; you will know why Hillary won or why she should have won.

The past is always a guide to the future and we have the benefit of two recent presidencies, one from a Republican and the other from a Democrat. One has served two full terms followed by the other whose second term will end in a few months. Accordingly, I have devoted chapters One and Two to examine the Bush and Obama presidencies. You will find that the information is based on real facts.

Current chaos in the Republican Party is examined in Chapter Three which includes facts as I could find them and my opinions that I hope you may agree with.

Chapter 4 is not for the faint-hearted. It's about Businessman from New York, Donald J. Trump.

In as much as most Republicans and some Independents yearn for the next president to be a Republican, the mere thought sends shivers among most Democrats and Independents. Having Trump as their nominee makes it scary.

I have made my case in Chapter 5 that Hillary Rodham Clinton should be the next president of the United States.

Hillary has been demonized by her political opponents for almost a quarter century based on accusations that have been proved to be false at every level. Such demonization is not good enough a reason to deny Americans of her services, not when she happens to be the most qualified for the job and the alternative is Donald J. Trump.

WC

CHAPTER 1

Presidency of George W. Bush

This is an exercise to examine some of President Bush's policies so as to determine the advisability of repeating them in a new administration in 2017. It is not an effort to praise or discredit his two terms even though, at times, it may appear as such when real events are described.

I haven't had the pleasure of knowing President George W. Bush personally, but have learned from those who have that it's impossible to dislike him, that he is a really nice kind guy who is fun to be with. This is absolutely true from what I have seen of him. Medicare Part D is a testament to the kind streak in him. In as much as he was fortunate to inherit a healthy economy and a nation at peace, he was faced with the worst attack on the homeland within the first year of his presidency. There can be no doubt that the policies he implemented were in good faith. The sole purpose of this chapter is to examine those policies in an effort to determine the advisability of repeating them in future administrations. Americans are a wise lot and hardly ever elect a bad person as their president. President George W. Bush is a god fearing good man.

 After a contentious election that required Supreme Court intervention to determine the outcome, George

W. Bush was inaugurated the President of the United States on January 20, 2001.

In addition to being the Commander-In-Chief the president is also the Guardian of the Economy.

Let's first examine how the economy fared under President Bush.

According to the Bureau of Labor Statistics of the United States Department of Labor the number of unemployed when Bush took office in January 2001 was nearly 6.0 million and the unemployment rate was 4.2 percent.[1] When Bush Left in January 2009 the number of unemployed was 11.6 million and the unemployment rate was 7.6 percent.[2] That was bad enough but the overall situation was far worse.

Following the bursting of the housing bubble in mid-2007, the United States entered a severe recession. The National Bureau of Economic Research (NBER) dates the beginning of the recession as December 2007.[3] There has been a debate among economists as to when exactly the recession started, but it is generally accepted that the country was in a recession in 2008.

By the fall of 2008, amidst a presidential and congressional election in progress, four major mortgage providers declared bankruptcy, and in September 2008, three of the largest financial institutions in the country namely AIG, Lehman Brothers, and Bear Sterns all collapsed. Soon, consumer banks started shutting down.

In mid-September Bush government bailed out American International Group Inc. (AIG) with $85 billion.

The Bush administration's $700billion emergency bail-out for the banking industry finally became law when President George W. Bush signed the bailout plan into law on Oct. 3, 2008. It was a controversial bill that created the Troubled Asset Relief program (TARP) and some members of both the Democratic and the Republican parties opposed the bill.[4] Main argument was that tax payer money should not be used to bail out Wall Street investment banks. Supporters of the bill argued that the plan would prevent further erosion of confidence in the U.S. credit markets, and that failure to act could lead to a depression.

When the bill first came to a vote on Monday September 29, 2008 in the House of Representatives, the lawmakers opposed it 228 to 205. Democrats voted 140–95 in favor of the legislation, while Republicans voted 133–65 against it.

The Market reacted swiftly to the vote. Following the vote, the Dow Jones Industrial Average experienced its largest single-day point drop ever; 777 points in a single day. The loss in market value was estimated at $1.2 trillion. The NASDAQ composite also experienced a severe loss, losing 9.1% in its third worst day ever.

On Wednesday, October 1, 2008, the Senate debated and voted on a revised version and the bill was passed by a margin of 74–25. Democrats voted 40-11 in favor of the legislation and Republicans voted 34-14 in favor of the legislation.

On Friday, October 3, 2008 the House voted on the revised version passed by the Senate and the bill was passed by a margin of 263-171. Democrats voted 172 to 63 in favor of the legislation, while Republicans voted 108 to 91 against it; overall, 33 Democrats and

24 Republicans who had previously voted against the bill supported it on the second vote.

I have included the voting record of the two parties in this instance to make the point that it was mostly the Democrats that helped President Bush to save the day. Most Republicans stuck to their ideology while the nation was experiencing a financial crisis.

The bailout of Citigroup and other large banks also began under the administration of George W. Bush.

The following is an accurate description of the state of the economy when President Bush left the White House in January 2009:

Employment crisis – Eleven point six (11.6) million Americans were out of work and the unemployment rate was at 7.6 percent. For the month of January 2009 alone, the jobs lost amounted to 598,000.

Housing crisis - According to a report issued in April 2010 by the Mortgage Bankers Association that looked at data between 2005 and 2008 more than 1.2 million households have been lost due to the recession.[5]   Thousands more home owners were facing foreclosure in 2009.

Financial crisis - By January 2009, Americans have lost trillions of dollars in stock market savings. Major financial institutions and private businesses have either already collapsed or were collapsing.

Budget Surpluses & Deficits – As to budget deficits, the U.S. government suffered budget deficits every year from 1970 through 1997 and finally recorded a surplus in 1998 under President Bill Clinton. There also were budget surpluses in 1999, 2000 and in 2001. 2001 was Clinton administration's last budget.

There was a budget surplus of $128.2 billion for the year 2001 when Bush took office. The budget deficit for 2009 when he left office was $1.413 Trillion.

The enormity of the crisis was such that on September 24, 2008 John McCain and Barack Obama, nominees for President of the Republican Party and the Democratic Party respectively, issued a joint statement describing their shared view that "The effort to protect the American economy must not fail."

Comparing the two terms of Bill Clinton with those of George W. Bush

What fairer way is there to do this than by examining the documents issued by the two administrations trumpeting their records?

The following is a copy of a letter from the Office of the Press Secretary dated January 7, 2000 released by the Bill Clinton White House depicting the Clinton-Gore economic record during their two terms from 1993 to 2001.[6]

THE WHITE HOUSE
Office of the Press Secretary

January 7, 2000

THE CLINTON-GORE ECONOMIC RECORD: THE LOWEST UNEMPLOYMENT RATE IN 30 YEARS

THE LOWEST UNEMPLOYMENT RATE SINCE 1969 AND MORE THAN 20 MILLION NEW JOBS. *In 1992, when Bill Clinton was elected President, the American economy was barely creating jobs, wages were stagnant, and the unemployment rate was 7.5* *percent. His bold, three-part economic strategy focused on three objectives: fiscal discipline, investing in education, health care, science and technology, and opening foreign markets. Today's jobs release provides more evidence that this strategy is working:*

The Unemployment Rate Was 4.2 Percent in 1999 – the Lowest Since 1969. *The unemployment rate was 4.1 percent in December bringing the average unemployment rate for 1999 to 4.2 percent – the lowest since 1969. The unemployment rate has fallen for seven years in a row. It has remained below 5 percent for 30 months in a row. For women the unemployment rate was 4.1 percent – the lowest since 1953.*

African American and Hispanic Unemployment Rates Were the Lowest on Record in 1999. *The unemployment rate for African Americans has fallen from 14.2 percent in 1992 to 8.0 percent in 1999 – the lowest rate on record. The unemployment rate for Hispanics has fallen from 11.6 percent in 1992 to 6.4 percent in 1999 – the lowest rate on record.*

20.4 Million New Jobs Created Under the Clinton-Gore Administration. *Since 1993, the economy has added 20.4 million new jobs. That's the most jobs ever created under a single Administration – and more new jobs than Presidents Reagan and Bush created during their three terms. Under President Clinton, the economy has added an average of 245,000 jobs per month, the highest of any President on record. This compares to 52,000 per month under President Bush and 167,000 per month under President Reagan.*

92 Percent – 18.8 Million – of the New Jobs Have Been Created in the Private Sector. *Since President Clinton and Vice President Gore took office, the private sector of the economy has added 18.5 million new jobs. That is 92 percent of the 20.4 million new jobs – the highest percentage since Harry S. Truman was President and presiding over the post-World War II demobilization.*

Most Rapid Growth in Construction Jobs In 50 Years. *After losing 662,000 jobs in construction during the previous four years, 1.9 million new construction jobs have been added during the Clinton-Gore years – that's a faster annual rate (5.1 percent) than any other Administration since Harry S. Truman was President.*

Fastest and Longest Real Wage Growth in Two Decades. *In the last 12 months, average hourly earnings have increased 3.7 percent – faster than the rate of inflation. This marks the fourth consecutive year of real wage growth – the longest consecutive increase since the early 1970s. Under President Clinton, real wages are up 6.5 percent, after declining 4.3 percent during the Reagan and Bush years. Real wage growth in 1998 reached 2.6 percent – the largest increase since 1972.*

Inflation–Lowest Since the 1960s. *Inflation remains virtually non-existent, with the underlying core rate of inflation at 2.0 percent this year – the lowest rate since 1965. In the last four quarters the GDP price index has risen 1.3 percent – the lowest rate of increase since 1963.*

- End of Letter –

The following is a copy of the letter released by the Bush White House depicting the Bush Record at the end of his second term: [7]

THE WHITE HOUSE

PRESIDENT GEORGE W. BUSH

THE BUSH RECORD

President Bush Helped Americans Through Tax Relief

President Bush Trusted Americans with Their Hard-Earned Money, Providing $1.7 Trillion In Relief Through 2008

President Bush demonstrated that letting people keep more of their own money leads to economic growth. *In 2001, America was experiencing the unprecedented triple shock of a recession following the dot-com bust, economic disruption due to the terrorist attacks of September 11, and corporate accounting scandals. Fortunately, the country was able to overcome these challenges, in part because President Bush's tax relief put more money in families' pockets and encouraged businesses to grow and invest. Following the President's 2003 tax relief, the United States had 52 months of uninterrupted job growth, the longest run on record.*

President Bush Signed The Largest Tax Relief In A Generation

President Bush's tax cuts provided $1.7 trillion in relief through 2008. *President Bush worked with Congress to reduce the tax burden on American families and small businesses to spur savings, investment, and job creation.*

In 2001, President Bush proposed and signed the Economic Growth and Tax Relief Reconciliation Act. *This legislation:*

* Reduced tax rates for every American who pays income taxes, including creating a new 10 percent tax bracket

* Doubled the child tax credit to $1,000 by 2010

* Reduced the marriage penalty beginning in 2005

* Put the death tax on the road to extinction

* Increased education tax benefits

* Increased limits on IRA and 401(k) contributions and changed limits on defined benefit pension plans – which were made permanent in the Pension Protection Act of 2006

In 2003, President Bush proposed and signed the Jobs and Growth Tax Relief Reconciliation Act. *This legislation:*

* Reduced the top tax rate on dividends and capital gains to 15 percent

* Accelerated income tax rate reductions

* Accelerated the expansion of the 10 percent bracket

* Accelerated the increase of the child credit to $1,000

* Accelerated the reduction in the marriage penalty

* Quadrupled small business expensing from $25,000 to $100,000

* Increased bonus depreciation for businesses to 50 percent through 2004

President Bush's Tax Relief Allowed Americans to Keep Trillions of Dollars Of Their own Money. Results of the President's tax relief were swift. The economy returned to growth in the fourth quarter of 2001 and continued to grow for 24 consecutive quarters. The economy grew at a rapid pace of 7.5 percent above inflation during the third quarter of 2003 – the highest since 1984. The President's tax relief reduced the marginal effective tax rate on new investment, which encourages additional investment and, in the long-term, higher wages for workers.

* In 2007, a family of four earning $40,000 saved an average of $2,053 thanks to the President's tax relief.

The President's tax relief was followed by increases in tax revenue. From 2005 to 2007, tax revenues grew faster than the economy. The ratio of receipts to GDP rose to 18.8 percent in 2007, above the 40-year average. Between 2004 and 2006, capital gains realizations grew by approximately 60 percent. Growth in corporate income tax receipts was especially strong in the President's second term, nearly doubling between 2004 and 2007 and contributing a full percentage point to the increase in the total federal receipts-to-GDP share.

The President's tax relief has shifted a larger share of the individual income taxes paid to higher-income taxpayers. With nearly all of the tax relief provisions fully in effect, the President's tax relief reduced the share of taxes paid by the bottom 50 percent tax payers from 3.9 percent in 2000 to 3.1 percent in 2005, the latest year of available data, *while increasing the share paid by the top 10 percent from 46.0 to 46.4 percent.*

President Bush Led The Response To The Financial Crisis Of 2008
The unprecedented economic growth was ended by the turbulence in the housing and credit markets, to which the President responded with bold action. President Bush *addressed the weakness in the economy early in 2008 by leading the bipartisan passage of an economic growth package that boosted consumer spending and encouraged businesses to expand, returning more than $96 billion to Americans. When the financial crisis intensified, President Bush led the passage and implementation of a rescue plan that helped address the root of the financial crisis, protected the deposits of individuals and small businesses, and helped enable credit to remain available to individuals and families. Moreover, he convened a summit with the leaders of the G-20 nations to discuss efforts to strengthen economic growth, deal with the financial crisis, reaffirm a commitment to free market principles, and lay the foundation for reform to help ensure that a similar crisis does not happen again.*

* The Administration warned of the risk that government-sponsored enterprises (GSEs) Fannie Mae and Freddie Mac posed to America's financial security beginning in 2001. *President Bush's first budget warned that "financial trouble of a large GSE could cause strong repercussions in financial markets." In 2003, the Administration began calling for a new GSE regulator. Despite resistance from Congress, President Bush continued to call for GSE reform until Congress finally acted in 2008 to provide* *the additional oversight the President requested five years earlier. Unfortunately, the reform came too late to prevent systemic consequences.*

- End of Letter –

For the record, the above letter by the Bush administration does not specify the number of jobs created during his two terms which is about three million jobs (net) in comparison to 20.4 Million New Jobs created during the Clinton Administration.

The following excerpt of a letter by the staff of The Wall Street Journal published on January 9, 2009 provides an explicit comparison of the record on jobs between Bill Clinton and George W. Bush.[8]

*"**The Wall Street Journal – Business***

*"**Bush On Jobs: The Worst Track Record On Record***

By WSJ Staff January 9, 2009

*President **George W. Bush** entered office in 2001 just as a recession was starting, and is preparing to leave in the middle of a long one. That's almost 22 months of recession during his 96 months in office.*

*His job-creation record won't look much better. The Bush administration created about three million jobs (net) over its eight years, a fraction of the 23 million jobs created under President **Bill Clinton**'s administration and only slightly better than President **George H.W. Bush** did in his four years in office."*

- End of Excerpt –

The economic record of President George W. Bush is pretty dismal and it's a good time to examine the policies he implemented that brought about such misery.

The following are a few of his policies for which he is directly responsible:

Bush tax cuts – How effective were they?

The letter by the Bush White House depicting his record boasts of the $1.7 trillion tax cuts he made during his presidency. He sure made those tax cuts, 50% of which benefitted the richest 5% of the American Tax payers.

Republicans strongly canvass tax cuts. They are committed to trickle-down economics. It's their contention that tax cuts to the rich leads to economic growth which will also benefit the middle-class and the poor. Is this really true? The effect of Bush tax cuts ought to provide answers.

Tax cuts made by the Bush Administration in 2001 and 2003 are collectively referred to as the 'Bush tax cuts.' These tax cuts were scheduled to expire at the end of 2010 and after a debate as to whether they should be allowed to expire or extended the Obama administration extended them for two years, the reason being that the country was just recovering from a severe recession and the recovery would be adversely affected if the tax cuts were allowed to expire.

Come 2012, Republicans argued that the Bush tax cuts ought not to be allowed to expire, that instead all those tax cuts should be made permanent. That wasn't the position of the Obama administration and the Democrats. The argument that ensued obviously included an examination of the merits or otherwise of the Bush tax cuts.

A report prepared for Members and Committees of Congress by the non-partisan Congressional Research Service dated July 18, 2012 titled The 2001 and 2003 Bush Tax Cuts and Deficit Reduction became a matter of contention by the Republicans because it found no correlation between top tax rates and economic growth, a central tenet of Conservative economic theory.[9] The following is an excerpt of the concluding remarks of this report:

- Start of Excerpt –

Concluding Remarks

The 2012 debate over the fate of the Bush tax cuts is likely to take place in an almost as bleak economic and fiscal environment as the 2010 debate over the fate of the Bush tax cuts. In the short term, the economy is growing slowly and unemployment is likely to remain over 8.5% for several more months. The long-term federal government fiscal situation is clearly unsustainable. The decision over the fate of the Bush tax cuts will affect the short-term economic situation and the long-term fiscal situation. The options will likely range from allowing all of the Bush tax cuts to expire after 2012 to temporarily or permanently extending some or all of the Bush tax cuts. **It can be argued that permanently extending all of the Bush tax cuts could make future tax reforms to deal with unsustainable deficits and debt trends more difficult.** *If the economy is still weak, a temporary extension would not harm the economy. Furthermore, allowing the high-income tax* *cuts to expire as scheduled could help reduce budget deficits in the short term without stifling the economic recovery.* **Research has shown that tax cuts directed to high-income taxpayers have a small simulative effect because they tend to save any additional income. Increasing tax rates for the richest 1% to 3% of taxpayers (by allowing the high-income tax cuts to expire) would likely neither significantly decreases consumer expenditures nor adversely affects short-term job growth. Increasing taxes to reduce long-term budget deficits after the economy has recovered, would likely have little negative impact on long-term economic growth and job creation.**

- End of Excerpt -

I have highlighted the remarks in the Conclusion that offended Republicans so much that they saw to it that the report was withdrawn by the Congressional Research Service.

Deregulating Wall Street was another Bush policy

This nation paid a heavy price for the Republican Party's obsession with deregulation. Sweeping financial deregulation and under-enforcement of existing rules under the Bush administration helped build the housing bubble and allowed financial institutions to pursue very risky trades unchecked. The result was the financial crash that plunged the nation into the Great Recession. Bush readily admits that substantial deregulation was enacted during his presidency but disputes that it was a major cause for the financial meltdown. There have been some outrageous denials on the same subject by several economists partisan to the Bush Administration. These don't even merit discussion.

The fact is that an act like *'The Dodd–Frank Wall Street Reform and Consumer Protection Act'* had to be passed in 2010 to give a semblance of confidence to the public that Wall Street will not be able to do in the future what they did during the Bush administration.[10] Dodd-Frank made major changes to the American financial regulatory environment. These changes affect all federal financial regulatory agencies and almost every part of the nation's financial services industry. This gave a semblance of confidence to the general public with reference to future activities of Wall Street. Nevertheless, there are those who still argue that even Dodd-Frank is not enough to prevent another financial crisis or more bailouts.

Not helping home owners struggling with their mortgages was an inexcusable policy of inaction by the Bush administration

There is little doubt that President Bush received terrible advice on this issue.

President George W. Bush came to office as a compassionate conservative and a born again Christian but did very little to help struggling homeowners. He had an obligation to help them for two very good reasons. One, from the time he assumed office he pushed hard to expand homeownership. Two, his policies led to the housing crisis.

The housing bubble burst in 2007.

In an effort to ease the housing crisis the House Financial Services Committee proposed legislation that would make it easier for homeowners to refinance their loans and stay in their homes. The committee estimated that the program could help 1.5 million homeowners who are having difficulty paying their mortgages. The Chairman of the committee Barney Frank explained that the millions of individuals who might face foreclosure because of the expanding credit crisis deserve help, even if they made a mistake by borrowing beyond their means, and added that if nothing happens and all those loans go under foreclosure, the economy would suffer even more.

Bush would have none of it. Instead, his administration touted existing FHA programs including the FHA Secure Plan the president announced in August 2007, calling them "simpler and more targeted" ways to help homeowners who are behind in their mortgage payments.[11] Unfortunately that proved to be insufficient and 3.1 million foreclosures were filed during 2008, up 81 percent from 2007 which meant that one of every 54 households received a notice in 2008. When Bush left office in January 2009 as many as six million homes were expected to go into foreclosure.

Bush Policy of weakening safety regulations and collective bargaining rights of workers

The Republican policy during the last few decades has been to oppose the very concept of workers unions.

President Bush, having taken office in January 2001 didn't take too long to start stripping away safety regulations and collective bargaining rights of workers.

The Occupational Safety and Health Administration (OSHA) has been in existence since early 1970s and served as the watchdog for worker safety at US job sites.[12] OSHA's job is to develop and enforce government standards that businesses and other non-governmental organizations are required to follow in order to prevent employees from getting sick or injured.

Just like several previous Republican administrations, President George W. Bush worked to lessen the regulatory power of OSHA and turn its mandatory worker-safety programs into voluntary-based efforts by employers.

According to government records, in 2005 there were more than 6,800 workplace-related deaths in the United States and 4,200,000 injuries and illnesses.

President Bush made no secret of his desire to limit new rules and roll back what he considered cumbersome regulations that imposed unnecessary costs on businesses.

Investigations by the *New York Times* and *Washington Post* have pointed out that the Bush administration has consistently scaled back OSHA regulations and enforcement efforts during his term.

According to the *New York Times*, OSHA has issued the fewest significant standards in its history during Bush's two terms in office. It has imposed only one major safety rule, and the only significant health standard it issued was ordered by a federal court.[13]

Furthermore, OSHA officials have killed dozens of existing and proposed regulations and delayed adopting others.

Across Washington, political appointees — often former officials of the industries they now oversee — have eased regulations or weakened enforcement of rules on issues like driving hours for truckers, logging in forests and corporate mergers.

"The people at OSHA have no interest in running a regulatory agency," said Dr. David Michaels, an occupational health expert at George Washington University who has written extensively about workplace safety. "If they ever knew how to issue regulations, they've forgotten. The concern about protecting workers has gone out the window."

According to a June 2004 report released by AFL-CIO, while Bush's economic policies have targeted the wages and security of working people, his union-busting efforts have tried to undermine the one tool we have available to protect ourselves - our unions.[14] Since taking office, the AFL-CIO reports, "Bush has waged a war against workers' freedom to form unions and have a voice on the job, often using the justification that collective bargaining is incompatible with national security." Simply put, Bush used rhetoric of "national security" to pursue the anti-union agenda he supported prior to the events of September 11th. In fact, Bush claimed that workers who wanted to preserve their collective bargaining right were opposed to national security and might be supporting terrorist efforts.

Bush's anti-union policies haven't been restricted to government action. The administration fought to allow the use of taxpayer dollars to fight unionization. When the former governor of California signed a bill that outlawed the use of tax money to fight unions, the Bush administration's National Labor Relations Board (NLRB) voted to intervene on behalf of a lawsuit brought against this bill by the Chamber of Commerce. Bush agreed that grants and subsidies made to businesses by states could be diverted from their stated purposes and be used to fight the right of workers to organize.

The following is an abstract of an article by ILR School of Cornell University released in 2010 under the title: Legal Protection of Workers' Human Rights: Regulatory Changes and Challenges in the United States.[15] It's a sad testament to President Bush's record of Union busting.

- Start of Abstract -

Cornell University
ILR School

2010

Legal Protection of Workers' Human Rights: Regulatory Changes and Challenges in the United States

Lance Compa
Cornell University, lac24@cornell.edu

Abstract

In a 2002 study, the US Government Accountability Office reported that more than 32 million workers in the United States lack protection of the right to organize and to bargain collectively. But since then, the situation has worsened. A series of decisions by the federal authorities under President George Bush has stripped many more workers of organizing and bargaining rights. The administration took away bargaining rights for hundreds of thousands of employees in the new Department of Homeland Security and the Defense Department. In the years before the 2009 change of administration, a controlling majority of the five member National Labor Relations Board (NLRB), appointed by President Bush, denied protection to graduate student employees, disabled employees, temporary employees and other categories of workers.

An October 2006, a NLRB decision was especially alarming for labor advocates. The NLRB set out a new, expanded definition of 'supervisor' under the section of US labor law that excludes supervisors from protection of the right to organize and bargain collectively. This exclusion has enormous repercussions for millions of workers who might now become 'supervisors' and lose protection of their organizing and bargaining rights. This case is discussed in more detail below in connection with a complaint to the International Labor Organization (ILO) Committee on Freedom of Association.

- End of Abstract –

War policies of President Bush

What happened on September 11, 2001 was a disaster the like of which this nation hasn't seen before. I am of course referring to the terrorist attacks on The Twin Towers in downtown Manhattan, New York; on the Pentagon in Arlington County, Virginia;

and the plane that crashed into a field near Shanksville, Pennsylvania. The blame for these cowardly acts falls squarely on the beast that passed off as a human being called Osama Bin Laden and his al-Queda terrorist organization.

A strange aspect of 9/11 is that we are now fifteen years in to the attack and are still not quite sure why we were attacked.

We were attacked by the same terrorist group prior to 9/11.

On February 26, 1993, a truck bomb was detonated below the North Tower of the World Trade Center in New York City. The intention was to send the North Tower crashing into the South Tower bringing both towers down and killing tens of thousands of people. It failed to do so but killed six people and injured more than a thousand.

Our embassies in Nairobi, Kenya, and Dar es Salaam, Tanzania were bombed by al-Qaeda operatives in August 1998 killing more than 200 people and injuring more than 5,000 others.

Our Navy warship USS Cole was bombed in October 2000 killing 17 sailors.

Given a half a chance they will attack us again and we still do not know why al-Queda hates us so much. For that I blame both Bush and Obama administrations. May be they know the real reason but it is so controversial or politically incorrect that they are reluctant to share it with us. The often touted reasons such as 'Muslims don't like our way of life' or 'they don't like Christians' or 'they are jealous because we are rich' are silly and insult our intelligence. Some have suggested that the presence of our military men and women on Arab soil is the reason why al-Queda hates us. This may be closer to the truth. All we the people can do is to hope that those who govern us either already know or will soon find out the real reason for this animosity. We need that knowledge to fight the war against terrorism successfully. Pretending that it is unimportant is no solution. The crazy talk by some Republicans that Obama refuses to say 'Islamic terrorism' is just that, crazy talk that will only add to the problem. The first thing that helps law enforcement to solve a crime is the motive and it is no different in terrorism related crimes.

War with Afghanistan

The reason for the Afghan war was 9/11.

The primary duty of a president of the United States is to protect and defend the homeland against enemies foreign and domestic. The Bush administration dropped the ball on 9/11 in that they didn't take the threat seriously in spite of intelligence (granted that dots were not fully connected) of a possible attack. Unfortunately, they were distracted by their preoccupation with Saddam Hussein's Iraq.

The following is an excerpt from the testimony of Richard A. Clarke before the 9/11 Commission.[16] He is the former National Coordinator for Security, Infrastructure Protection and Counter-terrorism for the United States.

Clarke worked for the **State Department** during the presidency of **Ronald Reagan** In 1992. President **George H.W. Bush** appointed him to chair the **Counter-terrorism Security Group** and to a seat on the **United States National Security Council**. President

Bill Clinton retained Clarke and in 1998 promoted him to be the National Coordinator for Security, Infrastructure Protection, and Counter-terrorism, the chief counter-terrorism adviser on the **National Security Council**. Under President **George W. Bush**, Clarke initially continued in the same position, but the position was no longer given cabinet-level access. He later became the Special Advisor to the President on cyber security. Clarke left the Bush administration in 2003.

- Start of Excerpt -

CLARKE: "I welcome these hearings because of the opportunity that they provide to the American people to better understand why the tragedy of 9/11 happened and what we must do to prevent a reoccurrence. I also welcome the hearings because it is finally a forum where I can apologize to the loved ones of the victims of 9/11. To them who are here in the room, to those who are watching on television: Your government failed you; those entrusted with protecting you failed you; and I failed you. We tried hard, but that doesn't matter because we failed. And for that failure, I would ask -- once all the facts are out -- for your understanding and for your forgiveness. With that, Mr. Chairman, I'll be glad to take your questions".

- End of Excerpt -

I just want to make it clear that neither President Bush nor his Administration were responsible for 9/11. He may have got his priorities wrong, but that in no way means that President Bush is to be blamed for the horrors of 9/11.

Getting back to the Afghan war let me state at the outset that I did not consider the war against Afghanistan was a necessary war. Political leaders of both parties including President Obama have taken the position that the Afghan war was necessary. I beg to disagree.

The legislation authorizing the Afghan war came to a vote in the House of Representatives on September 14, 2001. The House passed it with 420 ayes, 1 nay and 10 not voting. California Democrat Barbara Lee was the only member that voted against the bill.

Also on September 14, 2001 the U.S. Senate passed that legislation by roll call vote. The totals in the Senate were: 98 Ayes, 0 Nays, 2 Present. Not Voting were the Republican Senators Larry Craig of Indiana and Jesse Helms of North Carolina.

So you see, when I say that the Afghan war was unnecessary my only company was Congresswoman Barbara Lee. I am not even sure that we opposed the war for the same reasons. Following are briefly my reasons:

What we needed to do was to destroy Bin Laden and his terrorist organization al-Queda. At the aftermath of 9/11 the whole world was with the United States. Rumor had it that even Iran offered help to get Bin Laden. In as much as our intelligence failed to connect dots and prevent 9/11, the abilities of the CIA are no secret. If half the money spent just on preparing for the war against Afghanistan was made available to the CIA they would have found a way to destroy Bin Laden and his terrorist network. No country would have denied air space for our war planes to do what was needed. If our actions resulted in some civilian casualties, that would have been far more merciful than the mass casualties of a never ending war. We could have got the job done without an invasion that we knew was not going to be easy. Also, there were no guarantees that we could get Bin Laden and his terrorist network by invading Afghanistan. Indeed, it so happened that as we invaded, Bin Laden and most of his cahoots escaped to neighboring Pakistan. A main justification for the war has been that we were able to destroy al-Queda training camps in Afghanistan which is quite true, but we could have done the same without having to invade the country. Couldn't the Bush administration have anticipated the obvious, that the terrorists could escape? Failure to prevent 9/11 was bad enough but it's inconceivable that Bush rushed to war with Afghanistan without first considering all options, a damn war that we are still fighting. Close your eyes and imagine for a moment what the world would be like today if we destroyed al-Queda without invading Afghanistan.

None of that mattered, Bush wanted a war and Americans fell in line.

War with Iraq

The invasion and occupation of Iraq is considered the worst foreign policy disaster of the United States. Just as we still do not know for sure why we were attacked by al-Queda we still do not know for sure why we went to war with Iraq.

A book written by Pulitzer prize-winning journalist Ron Suskind: *The Price of Loyalty: George W. Bush, the White House and the Education of Paul O'Neill* includes revelations by the first Treasury Secretary of President George W. Bush that within days of his first inauguration he has expressed a desire to invade Iraq.[18] The following is from Suskind' book:

Paul O'Neil was George Bush's first Treasury Secretary.

What happened at President Bush's very first National Security Council meeting is one of O'Neill's most startling revelations.

"From the very beginning, there was a conviction, that Saddam Hussein was a bad person and that he needed to go," says O'Neill, He adds that going after Saddam was topic "A", 10 days after the inauguration and eight months before Sept. 11".

"From the very first instance, it was about Iraq. It was about what we can do to change this regime," says O'Neill "Day One, these things were laid and sealed."

As treasury secretary, O'Neill was a permanent member of the National Security Council. He says he was surprised at the meeting that questions such as "Why Saddam?" and "Why now?" were never asked.

"It was all about finding a way to do it. That was the tone of it. The president saying 'Go find me a way to do this,'" says O'Neill. "For me, the notion of pre-emption, that the U.S. has the unilateral right to do whatever we decide to do, is a really huge leap."

And that came up at this first meeting, says O'Neill, who adds that the discussion of Iraq continued at the next National Security Council meeting two days later.

Based on his interviews with O'Neill and several other

officials at the meetings, Suskind writes that the
planning envisioned peacekeeping troops, war crimes
tribunals, and even divvying up Iraq's oil wealth.

- End of information from Ron Suskind's book -

There you have it. George W. Bush entered office
wanting this war and not a word of it was mentioned
in his campaign for president.

'Bush lied and people died' is a slogan born out of the
Iraq war. This briefly is what happened.

After 9/11 Americans no longer felt safe in their own
country and the atmosphere was ripe for fear
mongering.

The main pitch by the Bush administration to sell the
Iraq war to the American people was that Saddam
Hussein had chemical and biological weapons and
may be even nuclear weapons that he planned to give
to Osama Bin Laden who will then smuggle them in to
the United States and kill tens of thousands of people.
Most Americans, not all, fell for it.

Additional reasons were canvassed to sell the war to
the world, that the intent was to remove a regime that
developed and used weapons of mass destruction,
that it harbored and supported terrorists, committed
outrageous human rights abuses, and defied the just
demands of the United Nations and the world. Still
more justifications suggested were that the war
would change the Middle East so as to deny support
for militant Islam.

Out of all of the above reasons and justifications, the
only one that proved anywhere near to be true was

that Saddam Hussein's regime did commit human rights abuses.

An obvious example of Bush's rush to war was the manner in which his Administration treated the United Nation's Inspectors who were in Iraq under a U.N. Resolution to determine whether Saddam Hussein had weapons of mass destruction or nuclear capabilities. Hanx Blix was the former head of the International Atomic Energy Agency, the IAEA. He was also the chief weapons inspector for the United Nations in the years between 2000 and the invasion of Iraq in 2003. In subsequent interviews he has stated that he was given a mere three days notice to evacuate the inspectors before the invasion and he was in fear that the Iraqis might take them hostage. It turned out however that Iraqis were helpful to get them out.[19]

One of the biggest scandals among the falsehoods that were promoted to justify going to war with Iraq was Bush's inclusion of the infamous 16 words in his Jan. 28, 2003 State of the Union address: " The British government has learned that Saddam Hussein recently sought significant quantities of uranium from Africa." This statement was based on a forged document by an Italian journalist referring to an alleged contract between Iraq and Niger for the import of uranium.

Another disgraceful and inexcusable twist in this saga was the warning on CNN's Late Edition by Bush's national security adviser at the time Condoleezza Rice. [20] "There is no doubt that Saddam Hussein's regime is a danger to the United States and to its allies, to our interests," she said. "We know that there have been shipments going… in to Iraq, for instance of aluminum tubes that really are only suited ... for nuclear weapons." She added "We don't want the smoking gun to be a mushroom cloud."

The bottom line was that Bush took this nation to a war that killed and maimed thousands of our own soldiers, destroyed the infrastructure of a country, killed hundreds of thousands of Iraqi civilians and created 4 million refugees, all for no valid reason.

The Watson Institute for International and Public Affairs of the Brown University has done a project on the cost of Afghanistan and Iraq Wars and the following are some of its findings: [21]

Over 6,800 US soldiers have died in the wars.

370,000 people have died due to direct war violence, including armed forces on all sides of the conflicts, contractors, civilians, journalists, and humanitarian workers.

210,000 civilians have been killed in direct violence by all parties to these conflicts.

7.6 million Afghan, Iraqi, and Pakistani people are living as war refugees and internally displaced persons, in grossly inadequate conditions.

I have been unable to find any reliable figures as to how many Vets have been wounded in Iraq and Afghanistan wars. The same Brown University Report states that over 970,000 Iraq and Afghanistan veteran disability claims have been registered with the VA.

Financial Cost

According to a study out of Harvard University in March 2013, the United States has already spent nearly $2 trillion on the wars in Iraq and Afghanistan.[22]

But that bill is only "a fraction" of the total war costs says Linda J. Bilmes who is the Daniel Patrick Moynihan Senior Lecturer in Public Policy at Harvard University.

She says in her report that the final cost of the Iraq and Afghanistan wars will be between $4 and $6 trillion — and most of those costs have yet to be paid.

"The single largest accrued liability of the wars in Iraq and Afghanistan is the cost of providing medical care and disability benefits to war veterans" says Miss Bilmes and adds that "The legacy of decisions taken during the Iraq and Afghanistan wars will dominate future federal budgets for decades to come."

WHAT COULD WE LEARN FROM GEORGE W. BUSH'S PRESIDENCY?

Blame me if you will for not elaborating on good deeds by the Bush administration. There definitely were many. Medicare part D was one. Americans will always be grateful to President Bush for the manner in which he galvanized and consoled this nation after 9/11. I doubt it could have been done any better.

However, the purpose of this chapter is to evaluate the advisability of repeating Bush administration's economic and war policies in the future. I'll leave it to you to make that evaluation. Please grant me that I have presented facts accurately.

CHAPTER 2

Presidency of Barack Obama

By the time the 2016 presidential election draws near, the nominees of the two major political parties would have informed the electorate of their vision for the future and their policies on major issues.

Nevertheless, the two-term presidency of Barack Obama will be lurking in the back of voters' minds as they enter the polling booth. In the subconscious will be the presidency of his predecessor George W. Bush.

Timing is always significant when writing a nonfiction manuscript, paramount when the writing is in reference to a future event with a date certain. November 8, 2016 is the relevant date for me. We would be in to the seventh year and the eleventh month of Barack Obama's presidency. This chapter examines the policies he implemented, and how they fared.

The background of a president almost always has an impact on how he or she would govern. With that in mind, I have started this chapter with some information on Obama's background and his election to office.

Obama's background

Barack Hussein Obama was born in Hawaii on August 4, 1961 to a Kenyan father and a White American mother. His parents were well educated. His father Barack Hussein Obama, Sr. had his college education in the United States, earning a B.A. in economics from the University of Hawaii and a M.A. in economics from the Harvard University. His mother Ann Dunham had her college education in the University of Hawaii, where she earned her bachelor's in anthropology and also her master's and PhD in anthropology.

Obama himself is well educated. Having enrolled first at Occidental College in Los Angeles for his freshman and sophomore years and then at Columbia University in New York City, he graduated from Columbia in 1983 with a political science major. Perhaps the first signs of his desire for public service surfaced, when upon graduation he accepted an offer to work as a community organizer in Chicago's largely poor and black South Side. His assignment as an organizer was to organize residents to pressure Chicago's city hall to improve conditions in the poorly maintained public housing projects. He concluded that in order to get things done with the complexities of a city bureaucracy he needed a law degree. He enrolled in 1988 at Harvard Law School, where he excelled as a student, graduating magna cum laude and winning election as president of the prestigious Harvard Law Review for the academic year 1990-1991.

I guess this is when his desire for public service really manifested over his personal interests. Instead of going in for a prestigious position in the legal circles, like for example a clerkship with a Supreme Court

Justice, he opted to return to Southside Chicago. After directing a voter registration drive aimed at increasing black turnout in the 1992 election, Obama accepted positions as an attorney with the civil rights law firm of Miner, Barnhill and Galland and as a lecturer at the University of Chicago Law School.

His political career started in 1996 as a state senator in the Illinois State Senate and became a leading legislator passing nearly 300 bills aimed at helping children, old people, labor unions, and the poor.

In November 2004 he was elected to the United States Senate as the Junior Senator from Illinois.

However, the highlight of Obama's career in 2004 was his keynote address at the Democratic National Convention where he referred to himself as a 'skinny kid with a funny name who believes he also had a place in America' and declared "There's not a liberal America and a conservative America. There's a United States of America. There's not a black America and white America and Latino America and Asian America. There's a United States of America." In the 2004 Democratic Party National convention John Kerry was nominated as the Democratic Party candidate for the presidential election in November 2004. John Kerry lost that election to President George W. Bush who was seeking a second term. In the 2004 United States senatorial election in Illinois Obama won in a landslide and became the United States Junior Senator from Illinois.

Obama was the fifth African-American Senator in U.S. history, the third to have been popularly elected, and the only African-American serving in the Senate until he resigned his seat in November 2008 in preparation for his new job as the 44th President of the United States.

In the United States Senate Obama distinguished himself as a rank-and-file Democrat and a Democratic Party loyalist. He was also an unabashed Liberal even though he may not agree with this labeling.

He recruited a team of established, high-level advisors which was unusual for an incoming first-term senator. It was perhaps an indication of his higher aspirations. Pete Rousea, a 30-year veteran of national politics and former Chief of Staff to Senate Democratic Leader Tom Daschle was his chief of staff. His policy director was economist Karen Kornbluh, former deputy chief of staff to Secretary of the Treasury Robert Rubin. His key foreign policy advisors included former Clinton administration officials Anthony Lake and Susan Rice, as well as Samantha Power, author on human rights and genocide. He was a member of the Congressional Black Caucus and chairman of the Subcommittee on European Affairs. During his only term as a United States Senator, Obama held assignments on the Senate Committees for Foreign Relations; Health, Education, Labor and Pensions; Homeland Security and Governmental Affairs; and Veterans' Affairs.

Obama's desire and ability to work with Senators of the opposite party was manifested in the bills he co-sponsored with Republican senators. He worked with Senator McCain from Arizona towards immigration reform and added three amendments to the Comprehensive Immigration Reform Act, which passed the Senate in May 2006, but failed to gain majority support in the U.S. House of Representatives. Likewise, he partnered with

Republican Senator Richard Lugar from Indiana and Republican Senator Tom Coburn from Oklahoma to successfully introduce initiatives bearing his name.

Obama also travelled widely as a United States Senator. As a member of the Senate Foreign Relations Committee, Obama made official trips to Eastern Europe, the Middle East, and Africa. In August 2005, he traveled with Richard Lugar to Russia, Ukraine, and Azerbaijan. Following meetings with U.S. military in Kuwait and Iraq in January 2006, Obama visited Jordan, Israel, and the Palestinian territories. His third official trip in August 2006 was to South Africa, Kenya, Djibouti, Ethiopia, and Chad.

I have no personal knowledge of this but I would have thought that by this time Obama was seriously considering a run for president in 2008.

After eight years of George W. Bush any qualified white Democratic candidate would have easily won the presidential election in 2008. That was a given. I wouldn't say the same of any qualified black Democratic candidate, particularly a one-term Senator. That was an unknown which surely must have factored in when Obama considered his run for president in 2008. It turned out that on balance he decided that a run was the right course to follow.

Battle for the nomination

The Primary process commenced with seven Democrats seeking the party nomination. Among them were four sitting United States senators: Hillary Clinton, Barack Obama, Joe Biden and Chris Dodd. Former United States Senator John Edwards, United States Representative Dennis Kucinich and Governor

Bill Richardson were the other three. By the end of January 2008 all but Hillary Clinton and Barack Obama either withdrew or suspended their campaigns.

Thus began a primary battle the like of which you don't get to see often. The choice between a woman and a black man as their nominee was a first for any major political party and the Democratic Party was creating history. Obviously they both wanted to win but theirs was a tough but spirited fight between two candidates who apparently respected each other.

I am not going to bore you with details of a primary that was fought eight years ago except for the memorable incident when Bill Clinton compared the candidacy of Barrack Obama to a 'Fairy tale'. Who could blame him? The following article by Kate Phillips in *The Caucus, the Politics and Government blog of the New York Times* under the title 'The Clinton Camp Unbound" and published on January 8, 2008 does justice to what happened: [1]

- Start of Article -

The New York Times

The Caucus
The Politics and Government blog of The New York Times

The Clinton Camp Unbound
By Kate Phillips, January 8, 2008

MANCHESTER, N.H. — On the eve of the primary, the Clinton campaign on several fronts seemed to well over with emotion, making us wonder as we reviewed those video moments whether the sentiments – ranging from anger to near despair to exhaustion – would be in evidence as returns came in Tuesday night.

It's been a tough few weeks for the Clinton campaign, as the realization sunk in that her lead had slipped away around here. It feels like the tightly spun machine has come a bit unwound.

We're not sure which episode from yesterday to highlight first, but we'll start with one that we haven't posted yet on The Caucus. And that's the outpouring of anger and insults by former President Bill Clinton in talking about his wife's chief rival, Senator Barack Obama, while at Dartmouth in the late afternoon.

He literally shocked his audience, by criticizing Mr. Obama and his campaign, pointing his finger and raising his already hoarse voice. In response to a question about the Clinton camp's pollster Mark Penn wrongly insisting initially that Mr. Obama had gotten no "bounce" out of Iowa, Mr. Clinton began by acknowledging that Mr. Penn had been wrong. Then he fired away, in a mocking tone:

"But since you raised the judgment issue let's go over this again. That is the central argument for his campaign. It doesn't matter that 'I' started running for president less than a year after 'I' got to the senate after the Illinois senate. 'I' am a great speaker and a charismatic figure and 'I' am the only one who had the judgment to oppose this war from the beginning – always always always."

… and then Mr. Clinton moved on to more about what he and the Clinton campaign have insisted over and over — that Mr. Obama has not received the same

scrutiny or criticism about the war and other issues that Mrs. Clinton has.

"It is wrong that Senator Obama got to go through 15 debates trumpeting his superior judgment and how he had been against the war in every year, enumerating the years, and never got asked one time — not once, 'Well, how could you say that when you said in 2004 you didn't know how you would have voted on the resolution? You said in 2004 there was no difference between you and George Bush on the war. And you took that speech you're now running on off your Web site in 2004. And there's no difference in your voting record and Hillary's ever since.'

"Give me a break. This whole thing is the biggest fairytale I've ever seen.

"What did you think about the Obama thing calling Hillary the senator from Punjab? Did you like that? Or what about the Obama handout that was covered up, the press never reported on, implying that I was a crook. Scouring me—scathing criticism over my financial reports. Ken Starr spent $70 million and indicted innocent people to find out that I wouldn't take a nickel to see the cow jump over the moon."

...

"But the idea that one of these campaigns is positive and the other is negative when I know the reverse is true and I have seen it and I have been blistered by it for months is a little tough to take just because of the sanitizing coverage that's in the media doesn't mean the facts aren't out there."

Mr. Clinton turned to take another question, walked along the stage and said, "Otherwise, I don't have any strong feelings about that subject."

It feels like part of the thematic message the campaign was putting out: Mrs. Clinton saying there were talkers and doers, to her having to walk back comments she made about Martin Luther King Jr.'s impact on civil rights legislation that literally diminished his historic role– (oh yeah, he was a great speaker but it actually takes a president to get things done). Then of course, her getting all misty-eyed much earlier yesterday as she talked about how committed she was to the campaign and to events.

Mr. Obama was asked about this outburst by Mr. Clinton earlier today. Courtesy of Jeff Zeleny, here's the reply: "I understand they're frustrated right now. I suspect that they'll both try to get back on track in terms of the strategy for them to do better than they feel they're doing right now."

As for Mr. Clinton's pounding away at Mr. Obama's war stances over the years, Mr. Obama said: "But I think Tim Russert answered Bill Clinton this morning. Every point that he raised was a question that had been answered _ had been asked and answered, not only on "Meet the Press" but repeatedly.

"It is a little frustrating for the president to _ the former president _ to continually repeat this notion that somehow I didn't know where I stood in 2004 about the war. He keeps on giving half the quote. I was always against the war. The quote he keeps on feeding back was an interview on Meet the Press at the National Convention when Tim was asking,

`Given your firm opposition to the war, what do you make of the fact that your nominee for president and vice president didn't have that same foresight.' And obviously I didn't want to criticize them on the eve of their nomination. So I said, `Well, I don't know what _ you know, I wasn't in the Senate. I can't say for certain what I would have done if I was there. I know that from where I stood the case was not made.' He always leaves that out.

"And you know, I understand why he's frustrated. But at some point since we've corrected him repeatedly on this and he keeps on repeating it, you know it tells me that he's just more interested in trying to muddy the waters than actually talk fairly about my record."

Mr. Obama hasn't commented on all the remarks made last night by Mrs. Clinton about Dr. King and L.B.J. and civil rights, et al.

We'll be back later with more reaction, we'd bet, as the primary results start rolling in.

- End of Article -

I selected the above article because it includes quotes from both Hillary Clinton's husband, the former president Bill Clinton, and from Barack Obama. It also depicts how hard the battle was between Hillary and Obama. Nevertheless, other than Obama attempting to score points over Hillary by repeating again and again that she voted for the Iraq war, there weren't any personal attacks or mud-slinging by either of them.

The Democratic Party primary was concluded when Obama received enough super-delegate endorsements on June 3 to claim that he had secured the simple majority of delegates necessary to win the nomination, and Clinton conceded the nomination four days later. Obama was nominated on the first ballot, at the August convention.

In as much as the 2008 Democratic Party primary was one for the ages, the Republican Party primary was the opposite. It was an uninteresting affair with little enthusiasm among most Republican voters and on March 04, 2008 the senior United States Senator from Arizona John McCain became the presumptive presidential nominee of the Republican Party. Election results from the caucuses and primaries held on March 4th got him the delegates needed to clinch the nomination.

Battle for the White House (2008)

Both McCain and Obama tried their best to run clean campaigns. Unfortunately, the same couldn't be said of the Conservative and rightwing talk radio hosts and some TV hosts, mostly from the Fox News Channel. Their vicious and brutal personal attacks on Obama started while he was still battling for the nomination and continued right up to the election. Rush Limbaugh, Glenn Beck and Sean Hannity were among the prominent many.

Rush Limbaugh

During the nomination process, Rush Limbaugh started playing a strange game which he called "operation chaos" of encouraging Republicans to vote in Democratic primaries wherever rules permitted. Initially he was encouraging them to vote for Obama and then when he realized that Obama may actually win, he started encouraging his listeners to vote for Hillary. I wasn't quite sure what exactly he was doing and it's a real possibility that he didn't either. Most of his listeners are a confused lot any way and that is exactly the way he wants them to be. His interest is in ratings for his show which is fine, except that in the process he does colossal damage. After Obama secured the nomination Limbaugh's attacks on him became brutal, filled with sarcasm and bordered on being racist. It continued five days a week, three hours a day.

Glenn Beck

During this period Glenn Beck was hosting *Headline News* at CNN and also had his radio program.

On at least one occasion he raised the possibility that Obama was the anti-Christ. On March 27, 2008 Glenn Beck had Christian pastor John Hagee on Headline News and the following is a part of what transpired: [2]

BECK: Let me ask you, I get so much e-mail on this and I think a lot of people do, and I have got a couple of seconds. They say Glenn, you and the media, you got to wake up. Barack Obama's making people faint and cry and everything else.

He is drawing people in. There are people – they say this about Bill Clinton – that actually believe he might be the anti-Christ. Odds that Barack Obama is the anti-Christ.

HAGEE: No chance. He has a lot of charisma. There's a media love affair with him right now. He is a very formidable political person. I believe the best leader for America in the future is John McCain.

BECK: Thank you very much, pastor. Back in just a second. That's good news at least where I stand.

On several occasions he claimed that Obama is a Marxist.

On August 4, 2008 Glenn Beck on his Headline News: *"The thing that I do find about Barack Obama is that -- and I think America is starting to catch on to this -- this guy really is a Marxist. He believes in the redistribution of wealth."* [3]

Sean Hannity

Sean Hannity didn't just dislike Obama, he hated him. It may not be appropriate for a third party to describe someone else's feelings towards another in those words, but unfortunately there is no other way to describe Hannity's undiluted animosity towards Obama. He left hardly any doubt that it was personal.

During the 2008 presidential election Hannity hosted a cable news show on Fox News Channel and a three-hour ABC Radio Networks program which was a nationally syndicated talk radio show that aired throughout the United States.

Hannity devoted his TV show and radio program more-or-less exclusively to demonize Senator Obama. After Obama clinched the Democratic Party nomination Hannity starkly explained: "That's my job. ... I led the 'Stop Hillary Express.' By the way, now it's the 'Stop Obama Express.'" He kept true to his words. He repeatedly portrayed   Obama as a dangerous radical. When he was not going after Obama, he attacked members of Obama's family.

The attacks against Obama took a distinct racist tone when some talk radio hosts and hosts at Fox News and ABC News channels started associating Obama with some sermons made by his former pastor Jeremiah Wright of Trinity United Church of Christ in Chicago.

The basis of their complaint was that Obama sat and listened to these sermons which contained racist statements against white people instead of challenging Wright or walking out of the Church. Obama's denouncement of the statements in question failed to settle this controversy and in an effort to settle it he gave a speech titled "A More Perfect Union", in which he sought to place Wright's comments in a historical and sociological context. Talk radio hosts continued to push this issue which got worse when Wright made a series of media appearances and made some controversial statements. It was finally put to rest when Obama spoke more forcefully against his former pastor, saying that he was "outraged" and "saddened" by his behavior and resigned his membership in the church.

Two other lines of personal attack against Obama

Personal attacks on candidates have unfortunately been far too common a feature in presidential politics in the United States. That is not to say that a candidate's personal character doesn't count. Far from it, character should make all the difference when deciding on the suitability of a candidate for the highest office in the world. It needs to be examined in minute detail. But the examination has to be based on facts. When assertions and insinuations on a candidate's character are based on total fabrications they become personal attacks. There were two such lines of personal attack on Senator Obama that are worthy of mention. One has particular relevance as it was promoted to the hilt by Donald Trump, the nominee of the Republican Party for the 2016 presidential election.

One such attack was meant to cast doubts that Obama was a Christian. The other was that he was born in Kenya and thus unqualified under the Constitution to hold office as the President of the United States.

Obama is a Christian, but that didn't count. On the one hand his critics were blaming him for being a member of Trinity United Church of Christ in Chicago, which is a Christian church, and on the other hand they were insinuating that he was a Muslim because his father was a Muslim and Obama attended school in Indonesia when he was a child. It started as a rumor and got legs when some Republicans started claiming it as fact.

Gen. Colin Powell, former Republican Secretary of State under President George W. Bush referred to questions about Obama's religion in an interview on NBC's *Meet the Press* prior to the presidential election in 2008.[4] What follows is an excerpt from that interview:

- Start of Excerpt -

"I'm also troubled by, not what Senator McCain says, but what members of the party say. And it is permitted

to [say] such things as, "Well, you know that Mr. Obama is a Muslim." Well, the correct answer is, he is not a Muslim, he's a Christian. He's always been a Christian. But the really right answer is, what if he is? Is there something wrong with being a Muslim in this country? The answer's no, that's not America. Is there something wrong with some seven-year-old Muslim-American kid believing that he or she could be president? Yet, I have heard senior members of my own party drop the suggestion, "He's a Muslim and he might be associated with terrorists." This is not the way we should be doing it in America.

I feel strongly about this particular point because of a picture I saw in a magazine. It was a photo essay about troops who are serving in Iraq and Afghanistan. And one picture at the tail end of this photo essay was of a mother in Arlington Cemetery, and she had her head on the headstone of her son's grave. And as the picture focused in, you could see the writing on the headstone. And it gave his awards -- Purple Heart, Bronze Star -- showed that he died in Iraq, gave his date of birth, date of death. He was 20 years old. And then, at the very top of the headstone, it didn't have a Christian cross, it didn't have the Star of David, it had crescent and a star of the Islamic faith.

And his name was Kareem Rashad Sultan Khan, and he was an American. He was born in New Jersey. He was 14 years old at the time of 9/11, and he waited until he can go serve his country, and he gave his life. Now, we have got to stop polarizing ourselves in this way. And John McCain is as non-discriminatory as anyone I know. But I'm troubled about the fact that, within the party, we have these kinds of expressions."

- End of Excerpt -

Well, that just about says it all but the story persisted and seven years later a CNN/ORC poll in September 2015 found that 29 percent of Americans, and 43 percent of Republicans, believe that Obama is a Muslim.[5]

Insinuations that Obama was not born in USA had no basis. It was pure invention. Despite the release of his official Hawaiian birth certificate the story persisted and came to be known as the 'Birther Movement.' Baseless as it was some polls suggested that at least one quarter of Republicans believed that they doubted Obama was born in USA.

Conspiracy theories and insults against Obama reached new heights after McCain announced Sarah Palin as his running mate. There is no doubt that Palin injected new energy and enthusiasm to McCain's campaign. She showed no hesitation to attack Obama personally and soon became a huge favorite of McCain supporters until she self-destructed at media interviews.

Obama's campaign

Senator Obama made sure that his campaign didn't make any personal attacks against Senator McCain who was a war hero and who was popular among both Republicans and Democrats.

Obama didn't have to go into lengths to assert how bad the economy was under the prevailing Republican Administration. Nor was it necessary to harp on the uselessness of the two Bush wars. By then most Americans had had enough of the two

Bush wars. All Obama had to do was to inspire confidence in the voters that if elected he would improve the economy and end the two wars. He did that in typical Obama fashion.

Obama's promises to the electorate were simple and straightforward: he promised hope and change.

He promised to turn the economy around by cutting taxes to the middle class and raising taxes on the very rich when the economy is in better shape.

He promised to end Bush's two wars and not to start any unnecessary new wars and to close Guantanamo Bay detention camp.

He promised to provide healthcare to all Americans.

Among other promises he made were to make improvements in the areas of women's rights, education, environmental protection, immigration and race relations.

The bottom line of the 2008 presidential election was that the conditions that prevailed made it nearly impossible for any Republican to be successful. The election was conducted amidst a severe recession in a country plagued by an economic crisis, a housing crisis, a financial crisis and two unending wars.

The election was Democrats' to lose and they could have lost it with a black man as their candidate, but Obama was too good a black man for that. He was a charmer and a phenomenal orator and enjoyed campaigning.

On November 4, 2008 Barack Hussein Obama won the presidential election in a landslide and on January

20, 2009 created history by being inaugurated the first African-American president of the United States.

On November 6, 2012 President Obama was re-elected for a second term also in a landslide.

Obama's two Terms as President

Obama's two terms will have a direct impact on who will be the next president of the United States

Winning an election could be fun, but assuming responsibility as the Commander in Chief of the mightiest military and the custodian of the largest economy in the world is something quite different.

Obama campaigned on 'hope and change.' However, having been elected, he first had to prevent the American economy from sliding into a depression.

The scope and intensity of problems that President Obama faced when he took office in January 2019 has often been said to be similar to those that Franklin D. Roosevelt faced in 1933. Was Obama up to the task? The answer is reflected in his re-election in 2012. Who succeeds him to the White House in January 2017 could assert it even more. Should a Democrat that promises to continue his policies were to follow him as president, Obama will be remembered as the charming young black prince that turned up at a cross-roads in our nation's history and guided it to a period of hope and peace.

Any recession is always bad, but it's dire when 11.6 million Americans have already lost their jobs and the economy was continuing to lose around a further 800,000 jobs a month. Top that with a housing crisis that has contributed to the loss of 1.2 million households with no end in sight in foreclosures and a financial crisis. It was hard to assess which crisis was worse. The financial crisis has cost Americans trillions of dollars in savings and major financial institutions were in a state of collapse. Then, there were the two unpopular and unending wars in Iraq and Afghanistan. Senator McCain, looking in, had to be muttering to himself "better you than me."

Obama understood that the situation demanded bold action and didn't hesitate. The following steps taken by his administration helped to turn the economy around and avoid a depression.

Stimulus Package (The American Recovery and Reinvestment Act of 2009) [6]

Obama's ability to obtain the best available advice served him well at the beginning of his term as president.

The nation needed cautious optimism and that is exactly what Obama provided when he candidly explained that the road ahead would not be easy – economic recovery requires work and dedication from all Americans.

"None of this will be easy. The road to recovery will not be straight. We will make progress and there may be some slippage along the way. It will demand courage and discipline. It will demand a new sense of responsibility that has been missing from Wall Street all the way to Washington. There will be hazards and reverses. But I have every confidence that if we are willing to continue doing the critical work that must be done -- by each of us, by all of us – then we will leave this struggling economy behind us, and come out on the other side, more prosperous as a people."

Those were his words at the signing of his initial economic stimulus package, The American Recovery and Reinvestment Act of 2009.[7] Congress approved the $787 billion plan on February 2009. The Act was an unprecedented effort to jumpstart the economy and save and create millions of jobs. Most important, it instilled the confidence needed to boost economic growth.

The stimulus package had three spending categories. It cut taxes by $288 billion. It spent $224 billion in extended unemployment benefits, education and health care. It created jobs by allocating $275 billion in federal contracts, grants and loans. Although it was a ten-year package, $720 billion (91.5%), was budgeted for the first three fiscal years and it did better than planned. By the end of FY 2009, $241.9 billion had been spent: $92.8 billion in tax relief, $86.5 billion in unemployment and other benefits and $62.6 billion in job creation grants.

Troubled Asset Relief program (TARP) [8]

To his credit President George W. Bush got through the Troubled Asset Relief program (TARP) in October 2008 which was a $700 billion emergency bail-out for the banking industry that helped prevent further erosion of confidence in the U.S. credit markets. Only a part of the funds were utilized during Bush's presidency.

Under the Obama Administration in February of 2009 regulators began performing "stress tests" on the nation's 19 largest financial institutions to test their financial health. This was an effort to see how much more money they needed to survive a steep economic downturn. The basic plan was to test the bank's assets against a pessimistic economic scenario so that regulators could establish whether the bank needed an additional capital buffer. All this was to prevent a recurrence of the catastrophic financial crisis.

The Homeowner Affordability and Stability Plan [9, 10]

The day after he signed the stimulus package, Obama announced a plan to help American homeowners refinance their mortgages or avert foreclosure. The plan which could ultimately cost as much as $275 billion was more ambitious and expensive than many housing analysts had expected and drew praise from consumer advocates as well as the financial industry. It would provide $75 billion in direct spending to keep people in their homes and the rest in additional financial backing for the government-controlled mortgage giants, Fannie Mae and Freddie Mac.

The plan had three components.

The first would help homeowners who were still current on their payments, but were paying high interest rates and could not refinance because they did not have enough equity on their homes, a problem that afflicted growing numbers of people as housing values tumbled.

A second component would assist people who were at risk of losing their homes. It would provide incentives to lenders who altered the terms of loans to make them affordable for the troubled borrowers.

A third component would increase the credit available for mortgages by giving $200 billion of additional financial backing to Fannie Mae and Freddie Mac.

As ambitious as the plan was, Obama administration officials cautioned that it could not possibly halt the tidal wave of foreclosures. Nor would it provide much help to millions of homeowners who were holding mortgages that were bigger than the market value of their houses. In his own words, this is how Obama explained the dire situation: "This plan will not save every home, but it will give millions of families resigned to financial ruin a chance to rebuild. It will prevent the worst consequences of this crisis from wreaking even greater havoc on the economy. And by bringing down the foreclosure rate, it will help to shore up housing prices for everyone."

Bailout of the Automobile Industry [11]

The bailout of Detroit's auto industry, General Motors, Chrysler Group and Ford really started in late 2008 under President Bush's Administration.

When Chrysler and General Motors were in danger of folding and sought help, President George W. Bush, to his credit, didn't turn his back on them. Denying help would have been the popular thing to do particularly among Republicans who were critical of using tax-payer money for any type of bailout. Instead, Bush agreed to a temporary bailout and provided GM with $13.4 billion in short-term financing through the Troubled Asset Relief Program. That was on December 31, 2008 and Bush was leaving office in less than three weeks on January 20, 2009.

Thus, the failing American Auto Industry became another problem that President Obama had to deal with as he was entering office. It was obvious from the outset that Obama was not willing to allow an iconic American industry to collapse under his watch, nor was he prepared to risk tax-payer money without adequate safeguards. He achieved both with a comprehensive bailout plan that allowed the companies to stay in business but imposed numerous conditions that would secure their viability and allow them to eventually return to profitability.

The bailout of the auto industry, just like the bailout of the financial industry was the subject of bitter controversy. The auto industry bailout plan involved the government taking over a controlling interest in the companies. In as much as Obama didn't want the government running car companies, the alternative was to let them go out of business right at the moment when the economy was reeling from the worst downturn since the Great Depression. At stake were not only the jobs of all of GM and Chrysler's employees, but the jobs of people who worked for hundreds of suppliers, from stereo manufacturers to steel and rubber producers. Estimates of the potential job losses topped one million.

So if you were an Obama supporter, or just a Democrat who didn't particularly care much for Obama, you still took the position that he did what had to be done.

If on the other hand you were a Republican, particularly a strong fiscal conservative, the auto bailout was part of Obama's government power grab, his insatiable desire to increase the federal government's control of the economy.

The federal government took over GM and Chrysler in March 2009 and ended its $80 billion bailout of the U.S auto industry on December 2014.

Following is a statement by President Obama on the auto bailout: [12]

"When I took office, the American auto industry – the heartbeat of American manufacturing – was on the verge of collapse. Two of the Big Three – GM and Chrysler – were on the brink of failure, threatening to take suppliers, distributors and entire communities down with them. In the midst of what was already the worst recession since the Great Depression, another one million Americans were in danger of losing their jobs.

As President, I refused to let that happen. I refused to walk away from American workers and an iconic American industry. But in exchange for rescuing and retooling GM and Chrysler with taxpayer dollars, we demanded responsibility and results. In 2011, we marked the end of an important chapter as Chrysler repaid every dime and more of what it owed the American taxpayers from the investment we made under my Administration's watch. Today, we're closing the book by selling the remaining shares of the federal government's investment in General Motors. GM has now repaid every taxpayer dollar my Administration committed to its rescue, plus billions invested by the previous Administration.

Less than five years later, each of the Big Three automakers is now strong enough to stand on its own. They're profitable for the first time in nearly a decade. The industry has added more than 372,000 new jobs – its strongest growth since the 1990s. Thanks to the workers on our assembly lines, some of the most high-tech, fuel-efficient cars in the world are once again designed, engineered, and built right here in America – and the rest of the world is buying more of them than ever before.

When things looked darkest for our most iconic industry, we bet on what was true: the ingenuity and resilience of the proud, hardworking men and women who make this country strong. Today, that bet has paid off. The American auto industry is back.

For our autoworkers and the communities that depend on them, the road we've taken these past five years has been a long and difficult one. But it's one we've traveled together. And as long as there's more work to do to restore opportunity and broad-based growth for all Americans, that's what we'll keep doing to reach the brighter days ahead.'

- End of Statement -

Even the diehard Obama haters will have a hard time to deny that the Stimulus Package (The American Recovery and Reinvestment Act of 2009), the Troubled Asset Relief program (TARP) started under President Bush, The Homeowner Affordability and Stability Plan, and the Bailout of the Automobile

Industry were responsible for the turning around of the economy.

Of course, economists, financial consultants, and all sorts of wizards affiliated with Republicans, Conservatives and Tea Partiers have tried desperately to punch a million holes on the bold and successful efforts by the Obama Administration to prevent the economy sliding into a depression. However, the problem they encountered was that Americans' memories were not that short. Americans remembered all too well the disaster that was handed over to Obama, a disaster caused by the failed policies of Republicans and Conservatives. Also these guys made the crucial mistake of forgetting that Americans are by and large a grateful people. Obama haters learned it the hard way at the 2012 presidential election.

Other Significant Accomplishments of the Obama Administration

In every presidential campaign the nominees of the two major parties and Independent candidates (if there were to be any) makes various promises to the electorate. Indeed, this is expected of them. A campaign that doesn't offer a candidate's vision for the future, his or her philosophy of governance and promises on major economic, social and foreign policy issues is not a campaign to be taken seriously. Not keeping those promises once elected makes fertile ground for voter discontent. The American electorate is neither stupid nor unreasonable. They soon find out when a candidate has made promises that he never intended to keep as president as against those that he couldn't deliver for reasons beyond his control. Americans are pretty good at separating the wheat from the chaff. With that in mind let's examine Obama's campaign promises and what he was able to accomplish.

Iraq war

Long before he came to Washington as a United States Senator, Obama opposed the Iraq war which he described as a 'dumb war'.

On March 19, 2003 President George W. Bush launched the invasion of Iraq.

During his presidential campaign in 2008, then-Senator Obama made a promise to end the war in Iraq, a pledge he reiterated again and again.

On January 21, 2009 his first full day in office, Obama directed his national security team to undertake a comprehensive review of our strategy in Iraq.

On February 27, 2009 as president he delivered his first speech on Iraq at Camp Lejeune, North Carolina. Following is an excerpt. [13]

"Next month will mark the sixth anniversary of the war in Iraq. By any measure, this has already been a long war. For the men and women of America's armed forces – and for your families – this war has been one of the most extraordinary chapters of service in the history of our nation. You have endured tour after tour after tour of duty. You have known the dangers of combat and the lonely distance of loved ones. You have fought against tyranny and disorder. You have bled for your best friends and for unknown Iraqis. And you have borne an enormous burden for your fellow citizens, while extending a precious

*opportunity to the people of Iraq. Under tough
circumstances, the men and women of the United
States military have served with honor, and
succeeded beyond any expectation."*

- End of Excerpt –

On April 7, 2009 President Obama made his first visit
to Iraq as Commander in Chief and said inter alia: [14]
*"It is time for us to transition to the Iraqis. They need
to take responsibility for their country and for their
sovereignty."*

On October 21, 2011 President Obama announced
that the United States will withdraw nearly all troops
from Iraq by the end of the year, effectively bringing
the long and polarizing war in Iraq to an end.
Following is an excerpt: [15]

*"THE PRESIDENT: Good afternoon, everybody. As
a candidate for President, I pledged to bring the war
in Iraq to a responsible end -- for the sake of our
national security and to strengthen American
leadership around the world. After taking office, I
announced a new strategy that would end our
combat mission in Iraq and remove all of our troops
by the end of 2011.*

*As Commander-in-Chief, ensuring the success of
this strategy has been one of my highest national
security priorities. Last year, I announced the end to
our combat mission in Iraq. And to date, we've
removed more than 100,000 troops. Iraqis have
taken full responsibility for their country's security.*

*A few hours ago I spoke with Iraqi Prime Minister
Maliki. I reaffirmed that the United States keeps its
commitments. He spoke of the determination of the*

Iraqi people to forge their own future. We are in full agreement about how to move forward.

So today, I can report that, as promised, the rest of our troops in Iraq will come home by the end of the year. After nearly nine years, America's war in Iraq will be over.

Over the next two months, our troops in Iraq -- tens of thousands of them -- will pack up their gear and board convoys for the journey home. The last American soldier[s] will cross the border out of Iraq with their heads held high, proud of their success, and knowing that the American people stand united in our support for our troops. That is how America's military efforts in Iraq will end."

- End of Excerpt -

On December 18, 2011 after almost nine years, the last U.S. convoy of American forces left Iraq thus ending the Iraq war.

For the American people, the ending of the Iraq war was a lot more than a fulfillment of a campaign promise by President Obama. For the families of over 4000 servicemen who made the ultimate sacrifice and thousands others who returned home seriously injured, the ending of this horrible war was a sigh of relief.

Gone are the days of national security and foreign policy being beyond partition politics and not surprisingly Republicans, Conservatives and Tea partiers periodically find fault with President Obama for ending the Iraq war. They do so without hesitation when they see any political advantage in doing so. I am not going to waste your time and mine by litigating the pros and cons of the Iraq war and the merits of ending it except to make one short statement – None of those who blame Obama for ending the Iraq war has the courage to suggest that American ground troops should return to Iraq, if indeed that is what they are yearning for. They are scared to even to make a small hint in that direction. They are trying to have it both ways. To me, that ends the argument.

Afghan War

In 2001 when al-Queda led by Osama bin Laden carried out the 9-11 attacks in United States, Bin Laden was living in Afghanistan where he also had his al-Queda training camps. Afghanistan was at the time under the control of Taliban that declined demands by the Bush Administration that they handover Osama bin Laden and expel al-Queda from Afghanistan.

On October 7, 2001 the United States with their ally the United Kingdom began bombing Afghanistan. It was the launch of Operation Enduring Freedom that started the Afghan war. The goal was to drive the ruling Taliban from power.

They were soon joined by other forces, including the Northern Alliance. In December 2001, the United Nations Security Council established the International Security Assistance Force (ISAF) to assist the Afghan interim authorities with securing Kabul.

NATO became involved as an alliance in August 2003 and later that year assumed leadership of ISAF with troops from 43 countries. NATO members provided the core of the force. One portion of U.S. forces in

Afghanistan operated under NATO command; the rest remained under direct U.S. command.

The initial mission was partially successful in that the Taliban was toppled quickly, and even though Osama bin Laden escaped to Pakistan with most of his terrorists, they were no longer able to have training camps in Afghanistan and were constantly on the run or in hiding which made it hard for them to organize new attacks.

Since then the U.S. and its allies have remained in Afghanistan trying to build up Afghan military and police forces sufficient to defend their country without outside help.

A major drawback of this war has been the inability of the US and allied forces to soundly destroy Taliban. Taliban have been able to periodically reorganize and launch attacks on Afghan governments elected subsequent to the invasion. This has seriously hampered efforts to rebuild core institutions of the Afghan state.

This was more or less the situation on ground in Afghanistan when Obama took over as president in January 2009.

During his 2008 campaign Obama promised to send more troops to Afghanistan. The purpose was to stabilize the Afghan government and having done that to end the war.
Like he promised he did in 2009 increase the U.S. troop presence in Afghanistan coupled with a timetable for the withdrawal of the foreign forces from Afghanistan beginning in 2011. The plan was for

security responsibilities to be gradually handed over to the Afghan military and police.

On December 2014 the United States and NATO formally ended their war in Afghanistan even though the insurgency they fought for 13 years was not totally destroyed. This made it necessary for some NATO and Unites States forces to remain in Afghanistan in a supporting role. This constituted a 13,000-strong residual force including 9,800 US troops for training and counter terrorism operations.

In October 2015 President Obama announced that he will maintain troop numbers at 9,800 for most of 2016 and about 5,500 troops will still be in the country when he leaves office in 2017.

This is where we are as of May 2016 on the Afghan war that started 14 years ago.

Eliminated Osama bin Laden

On May 12, 2011 nearly ten years after 9/11, President Obama addressed the nation to announce that a small team of Americans carried out an operation that killed Osama bin Laden, the leader of al-Queda. Following are a few excerpts of the remarks made by the president: [16]

"Tonight, I can report to the American people and to the world that the United States has conducted an operation that killed Osama bin Laden, the leader of al Qaeda, and a terrorist who's responsible for the murder of thousands of innocent men, women, and children."

"It was nearly 10 years ago that a bright September day was darkened by the worst attack on the American people in our history. The images of 9/11 are seared into our national memory –"

"Today, at my direction, the United States launched a targeted operation against that compound in Abbottabad, Pakistan. A small team of Americans carried out the operation with extraordinary courage and capability. No Americans were harmed. They took care to avoid civilian casualties. After a firefight, they killed Osama bin Laden and took custody of his body."

"For over two decades, bin Laden has been al Qaeda's leader and symbol, and has continued to plot attacks against our country and our friends and allies.

The death of bin Laden marks the most significant achievement to date in our nation's effort to defeat al Qaeda."

- End of Excerpt -

Dodd Frank

The Dodd–Frank Wall Street Reform and Consumer Protection Act (commonly referred to as Dodd-Frank) passed by the Obama Administration in 2010 was an attempt to prevent the recurrence of events that caused the 2008 financial crisis.[17]

The scale and severity of the crisis was unlike any seen in generations and resulted in trillions in lost wealth. Even worse, it left millions of Americans unemployed. A broken financial regulatory system that allowed large parts of the finacial system to operate with little or no oversight was a principal cause of that crisis. It was a system that allowed mean lenders to use hidden fees and fine print to take advantage of consumers.

The purpose of Dodd-Frank was to prevent the excessive risk-taking by Wall Street that led to the financial crisis. The law also provid common-sense protections for American families. reated a new consumer watchdog to prevent moage companies and pay-day lenders from exploitinconsumers.

Dodd-Frank established several ngovernment agencies.

For example, the Financial Stabilityersight Council and Orderly Liquidation Authority ntors the performance of companies deemeo big to fail" in order to prevent a widespread ecolc collapse.

The council can break up large banat may pose a risk to the financial system becaut their size. It can also quickly and neatly liquidatestructure firms it deems too financially weak.

The Orderly Liquidation Fund provioney to assist with the liquidation of financipanies that have been placed in receivership be of their financial weakness.

The new Federal Insurance Office is and monitors insurance companies that se a systemic risk.

The new Consumer Financial Proteureau (CFPB) is responsible for preventinory mortgage lending, improving the claortgage paperwork for consumers and reducntives for mortgage brokers to push home buyers into more expensive loans. The Bureau has also changed the way credit card companies and other consumer lenders disclose their terms to consumers. It requires loan terms to be presented in a new, easy-to-read-and-understand format.

Another key component of Dodd-Frank is the Volcker Rule that restricts the ways banks can invest and regulates trading derivatives.

The new SEC Office of Credit Ratings is given the task to improve accuracy of ratings provided by the agencies that evaluate the financial strength of businesses and governments.

As with each and every action taken by the Obama Administration Dodd-Frank became a lightning rod, too much regulation for some and not enough for others.

As to be expected many in Wall Street see Dodd-Frank as an overreaction to the recession of 2008, one that will burden financial institutions with cumbersome rules and deter overall economic growth.

Others see it as necessary to protect investors and reduce unnecessary risk as well as to protect consumers.

Those in favor of the bill say that had the rules been in place, the recession might not have happened.

Harsh critics of Wall Street believe that the regulations don't go far enough to reign in an out-of-control Wall Street bent on taking risks and then being bailed out with public tax dollars.

Obamacare (The Patient Protection and Affordable Care Act (PPACA) 2012, commonly called the Affordable Care Act (ACA) 2012) [18]

It isn't easy to devise a system that provides adequate healthcare to over 300 million people. That, however, is not an excuse for an unfair system which is what we had prior to Obamacare. It failed to provide even basic insurance coverage to millions of Americans. For decades, leaders of the Democratic Party have been trying to find solutions. Republican Party leaders on the other hand were willing to contend with the status-quo. It was hard to even get them to accept that there was a problem. Before Obamacare they used to say that 'we have the best health care system in the world'. It was as if the 40 million uninsured didn't exist. Obamacare made them change their stance just a little. They hate Obamacare so much that they are now willing to at least pay lip-service to alternatives.

According to the 2014 annual report of the United States Census Bureau on health insurance coverage, 13.3 percent of the population or 41.8 million people were uninsured in the United States in 2013, the year before the implementation of President Obama's health care law.[19] Reports by the Census bureau are considered the most reliable and hence most widely-cited.

How did it happen that more than one in thirteen people in the United States were without health insurance? The uninsured figures for adults between 19 years and 64 years gets much worse because most children under 19 years and seniors over 65 years who didn't have private insurance had some form of government insurance, Medicaid or Medicare.

According to the Keiser Family Foundation almost 41 million out of the 41.8 million uninsured in 2013 were nonelderly Americans.[20] I find these people falling into three main categories:

(1) Those who could afford to buy health insurance but consciously decided not to because they felt they didn't need it. These were mostly young and middle-aged healthy people who believed that the risk of them falling ill or meeting with an accident were so low that they would chance it. Of course they were also aware of the option of emergency hospitals. These were the free riders, selfish and irresponsible. It's hard to sympathize with them when they catch a nasty disease.

(2) Those who wanted to buy, but simply couldn't afford health insurance due to financial reasons. They needed help.

(3) Those who could afford and wanted to buy health insurance but were denied by the health insurance companies for various reasons such as pre-existing conditions. This clearly was a horrible situation that needed to be rectified.

The Affordable Care Act deals with all three of these categories.

The mandatory requirement to buy health insurance took care of the first category. This group didn't protest half as much as the Obama haters who were hysterical that their freedoms under the constitution were being violated. The government cannot force a citizen to buy anything, they argued, but the Supreme Court decided 'yes they can' and that settled that. It's worth mentioning that a major organization of the Conservatives, The Heritage Foundation, promoted the very same concept of healthcare mandates not too long ago and the Republicans were all for it, but this now was a proposal by President Obama and how could he possibly propose anything good?

Those in category two, at least in my view, had the worst of both worlds. They were not rich enough to pay for health insurance and were not poor enough to qualify for a government program. These folks needed help and the ACA made provisions for them to get coverage mostly by extending Medicaid. This dismayed Republicans. They complained that these provisions will increase premiums for everybody and argued that poor people could always go to the emergency hospitals. It mattered less to the compassionate Conservatives that some of these people haven't been to a Doctor in their lifetime, that most of them have never had any kind of preventive care, and that annual checkups is a notion foreign to them. The sad fact is that the vast majority of Republican Governors have refused to extend Medicaid to the poor in their states. They declined millions of federal dollars available to their states under the ACA for the purpose of extending Medicaid to the poor. The puny excuse is that their states will have to contribute a very small percentage of the cost, not now, but in the future after several years.

Now we come to the third category. The insurance companies did as they pleased in providing health insurance. They almost always refused to insure people with pre-existing conditions. Insurance companies had no problem dropping insured already in their plans when they needed help most. They increased co-pays and premiums as much as they could get away with. Basically the insurance companies were a law unto themselves. It's hard to believe that even Tea Partiers would have tried to defend these actions by the insurance companies, but they really tried. I have heard Tea partiers claiming that these folks should have obtained insurance before they got sick. Well, the ACA took care of this problem too. No more can insurance companies deny insurance because of a pre-existing condition.

This is the bottom line. According to their 2015 annual report of the United States Census Bureau on health insurance coverage, the percentage of people without health insurance coverage for 2014 was 10.4 percent or 33.0 million. This was a decrease in the uninsured rate by 2.9 percent or 8.8 million between 2013 and 2014 – a direct result of the Affordable Care Act 2012.[19]

Obama Administration received no help from the Republicans in the implementation of The Affordable Care Act. On the contrary, the Republican majority in the House of Representatives has voted more than 50 times to repeal the Affordable Care Act or some part of it. They have twice brought challenges to the ACA in the Supreme Court only to be rebuffed both times. They even caused a government shutdown in an effort to defund the ACA.

Republican governors of 23 states have refused Medicaid expansion under ACA denying thousands of poor folk the opportunity to get health insurance. All these obstructions by the Republicans, Conservatives and Tea Partiers notwithstanding, a report by the Commonwealth Fund concludes that as of May 1, 2014 about 20 million Americans have gained coverage under the Affordable Care Act.[21] The report looks at both people who gained coverage through insurance marketplaces, and people who gained coverage due to provisions in the Affordable Care Act such as those qualifying for Medicaid and those now covered through the Children's Health Insurance Program. They estimate that 7.8 million people under the age of 26 who were allowed to be covered as dependents on their parents' plans under the ACA have in fact enrolled. The report further adds that that 8 million people were enrolled in coverage via new health insurance marketplaces and five million purchased coverage directly from insurers.

The Affordable Care Act is working and could be improved to cover all uninsured Americans if only our politicians really cared.

Overhaul of the Federal Student Loan Program

A centerpiece of President Obama's education agenda, this is one of the least talked about but most important changes brought about by the Obama Administration.

It removed banks out of the Federal Student Loan Program and *expanded Pell Grant Spending.* It was easily said than done and ended one of the fiercest lobbying fights in Washington. Forcing commercial banks out of the federal student loan market that cut off billions of dollars in their profits was not easy. It was included in the final health care package and Republicans unanimously opposed it in both chambers.

The basis of the whole program as it existed was hard to understand. Since the loan program began in 1965, commercial banks have received guaranteed federal subsidies to lend money to students, with the government assuming nearly all the risk. It fattened the bottom line for banks at the expense of students and taxpayers.

The changes provided a huge infusion of money to the Pell grant program and offered new help to lower-income graduates. Republicans described it as a government take over.

Global Leadership on Climate Change

Climate change is irreversible which makes it far more haunting than other horrors plaguing the world. Glaciers that melt cannot be easily refrozen; coastal cities once flooded are unlikely to be rebuilt; extinct species are gone forever. I have little doubt that when Senator Obama referred to 'the urgency of now' in his 2008 campaign he had climate change also in his mind. His climate strategy began with the infusion of $90 billion in green-energy financing in the stimulus package. That was within weeks into his presidency.

What needs to be done to comprehensively battle climate change is nowhere near being fully accomplished. Nevertheless, the December 2015 Paris Accord was huge when representatives of 195 nations reached a landmark accord to lower planet-warming greenhouse gas emissions.[22] President Obama spoke of the deal in a televised address from the White House. "This agreement sends a powerful signal that the world is fully committed to a low-carbon future," he said. "We've shown that the world has both the will and the ability to take on this challenge."

Scientists say that the Paris Talks represented the world's last, best hope of striking a deal that would begin to avert the most devastating effects of a warming planet. They add that the Paris Accord will not, on its own, solve global warming but it will cut global greenhouse gas emissions by about half as is necessary to stave off an increase in atmospheric temperatures which otherwise will lead to rising sea levels, severe droughts and flooding, widespread food and water shortages and more destructive storms.

Iran Nuclear Deal

War, war and more war is what the Republicans and Conservatives seem to want. President George W. Bush invaded two Arab countries a mere three years into his presidency, and since then all hell has broken loose in that part of the world. Even with that background the current crop of Republicans are desperate to go to war with Iran.

Senator Obama was soundly criticized by Republicans and some Democrats back in his 2008 campaign for his willingness to negotiate with Iran to keep Iran from acquiring a nuclear weapon. He argued that a big mistake the Bush administration made was being unwilling to talk to enemies. Neither President Obama nor the Republicans and some Democrats changed their position for the next seven years.

President Obama pursued a policy of persuading and at times coercing other countries to strengthen sanctions against Iran while always publicly maintaining that he was willing to negotiate with Iran to bring about a peaceful solution if Iran was willing to abandon efforts to acquire a nuclear weapon. It worked. The United States with other major powers, including China and Russia were able to put crippling economic sanctions on Iran to pressure the country to abandon its nuclear program. The Iranians finally came to the table to negotiate to remove those sanctions in exchange for a dismantling of the nuclear program and an ongoing regime of inspections.

In July 2015 six world powers, including the United States, struck a landmark nuclear deal with Iran. "We succeeded in forging a strong deal to stop Iran from obtaining a nuclear weapon" is how President Obama announced the Accord.[23]

U.S. – Cuba Relations

The deterioration of the relationship between the United States and Cuba was rapid. It all started with the Cold War.

Fidel Castro seized power in Havana with the 1959 Cuban Revolution. Castro's communist political ideology was no secret. Nevertheless, the United States recognized his government but it didn't take long for the relationship to go south. It soon became apparent that Castro's heart was with the Soviet Union when he nationalized U.S.-owned properties, and hiked taxes on American imports. Washington retaliated by instituting a ban on nearly all exports to Cuba which was expanded into a full economic embargo and stringent travel restrictions.

The United States severed diplomatic ties with Cuba in 1961 and we had the Bay of Pigs invasion also in 1961 followed by the Missile Crisis in 1962. That was about it. Ever since, economic embargo and diplomatic isolation was the U.S. policy toward Cuba which really didn't help to improve the lives of Cubans.

President Obama was not willing to accept the status quo. In August 2015 the U.S. reopened its embassy in Cuba, the first symbolic step to normalizing relations between the two countries and the first time the American flag has flown in Havana in 54 years.

"We turned the page on an outdated, half-century-old policy by re-establishing diplomatic relations with Cuba and reopening embassies in both our countries, allowing us to build greater ties between Americans and Cubans," said President Obama in announcing the new U.S. - Cuba relations.

Since the momentous occasion, the Obama Administration has taken further steps to make it easier to travel to and do business in Cuba.

The U.S. Supreme Court

The importance of the United States Supreme Court, a co-equal branch of our government needs no emphasis.

President Obama deserves credit for having nominated and obtained confirmation for Sonia Sotomayor, the first Hispanic and third woman to serve, in 2009; and Elena Kagan, the fourth woman to serve, in 2010. They replaced Justices David Souter and John Paul Stevens, respectively.

President Obama has nominated Appeals Court Judge Merrick Garland to the U.S. Supreme Court on March 2016 to fill the seat vacated by the sudden death of Justice Antonin Scalia.

Judge Garland is a highly regarded jurist who is the chief judge of the U.S. Court of Appeals for the

District of Columbia Circuit and has been on the appellate bench for almost two decades.

Republicans who hold the majority in the senate have so far declined to hold hearings on the nomination of Judge Garland. They say that it has to be left for the next president to nominate a Justice to fill the seat vacated by Justice Scalia.

Some Republicans for the last seven years have had a hard time in accepting that we do have a president and that his name is Barack Obama.

America's Image Abroad

President George W. Bush presided over the most catastrophic collapse of America's reputation since world war two.

He got America embroiled in two wars, one of which, the Iraq war was launched against the tide of world opinion. World citizenry was never given a reasonable explanation as to why we invaded Iraq, the simple reason being that there was no good reason.

It was made worse when the Bush White House ignored international agreements, such as the Geneva Convention that banned torture and created a secret system of detention that was unmasked when photos made their way to the American media. It's hard to forget how suspected terrorists were captured and tortured in Baghdad's Abu Gharib prison.

Reversing the sharp decline in world opinion toward the United States was an undertaking that President Obama embraced enthusiastically.

A mere two days after taking office Obama nullified Bush-era rulings that had allowed detainees in U.S. custody to undergo certain "enhanced" interrogation techniques considered inhumane under the Geneva Conventions. With new policies and diplomacy, he reversed the decline in world opinion toward the United States.

Republicans gleefully contend that Obama has ruined America's standing in the world. Ha! Ha! They say it but one wonders if they believe it themselves?

You must have got used to it by now. Each and every action taken by the Obama Administration has been thrashed and ridiculed by the Republicans, Conservatives and Tea partiers quite irrespective of the merits of those actions. It was kind of funny at the start but soon became a serious obstruction for progress.

The Election is getting closer and it's time to see what's up with the GOP?

CHAPTER 3

CHAOS IN THE GOP

If Barack Obama didn't win the presidency in 2008, there wouldn't have been a Tea Party movement. Tea Party is partly responsible for the chaos in the Republican Party. When you become the majority party you are expected to govern. Being a 'party of no' is not an option. Republican leaders ought to have seen it coming, the writing was on the wall.

The Myth about an Angry Electorate

In this election season 'Angry Electorate' is the favorite term of politicians. When Republicans cannot handle Donald Trump, they cite the angry electorate. When Bernie Sanders did better than expected against Hillary Clinton the reason given was the angry electorate. Political pundits and news casters also turn to the angry electorate when they haven't the courage to report what's really going on. Well, not me, I don't believe in any new vast angry electorate.

There certainly are the hate filled angry Tea Partiers. They have been around since 2008. In addition, there are also quite a few Republicans who are unhappy with their leadership. Together they make up Trump's diehard supporters. There are hardly any Democrats that support Trump. Not even a significant handful. Those Democrats who were looking for radical change and were with Bernie will be in Hillary's corner come election date. If you have been watching T.V., it doesn't matter which channel, you would think that the Democrats are fighting to get in line to vote for Trump.

Let's see what happened at Trump rallies. Trump calls Mexicans rapists, wants to ban Muslims from entering the country, wants to round up and deport thirteen million undocumented immigrants and his crowds roared their approval. You know why? These promises are the exact opposite of what Obama stands for, and are now being made by the very same Trump who kept the *'Birther Movement'* alive for years and years. As you may know *the Birther Movement* refers to those who believe that Obama was not born in the United States and is therefore ineligible to be president. Trump's supporters mostly are the Tea Partiers. Their core is the hatred for Obama, the pretences are the supposed objections to free trade, undocumented immigrants, excessive spending, national debt and the like. They also despise the Republican leaders, the so called Establishment Republicans for having failed to stop Obama. Donald Trump is their new leader, their savior. They support Trump no matter what. Trump once said that he could stand on Fifth Avenue and shoot people and his supporters will still be with him and he is right. As long as Tea Partiers know that Trump hates Obama the bond will be solid.

Trump says the most atrocious things about women. When he was the GOP front runner he tweeted a picture of the wife of his nearest rival Ted Cruz after having distorted her picture to look really ugly. Alongside that he placed a beautiful picture of his own wife. The purpose was to get under Ted Cruz's skin.

For most Americans, this was disgusting behavior, but not for Trump supporters. They loved it.

He claims that the countries we trade with, particularly China, Japan and Mexico are robbing us. He wants Japan and South Korea to get their own nuclear arsenal because Americans are tired of defending them. These were some of the slogans at his rallies and the crowds went wild.

A few guys from Black Lives Matter were protesting at Trump's rallies and his crowds more or less physically kicked them out at Trump's urging. His campaign had no regrets and indeed they benefitted by such incidents.

Trump voters also hate Hillary Clinton. No surprise there. Hillary has embraced Obama. They felt differently towards Bernie Sanders. They seemed to like Bernie and some have said they would even vote for Bernie in the general election if their guy Trump is not on the ballot. Now here is the kicker: Bernie's policies are the exact opposite of what the Tea Partiers say they are fighting for; Bernie's are Obama's policies on steroids; but the Tea Partiers are fine with those policies as long as Obama isn't there as president.

 Mainstream media, Drive-Bys as Rush Limbaugh calls them, have never had the courage to expose Tea Partiers for who they really are. That would be too racially sensitive for the media, even for those supposed to be left leaning like the MSNBC. The Tea Partiers have the best of both worlds. They have Fox News in their pocket and the rest of the media running scared. Tea Partiers are bit quiet as of now, but make no mistake, they will be around in their elements closer to the election date.

Where do the Ultra Conservatives fit in all this?   Ultra Conservatives are Republicans on the far extreme end of the right. They form a substantial section of the modern Republican Party. To them 'compromise' is a bad word and it's always their way or the highway. There were no signs during the primary that they were an angry lot. They just want their guy in the White House so as to implement their ultra right-wing agenda.

So you see, there is no such thing as the 'angry electorate' unless you call the Tea Partiers and a few other Republicans the electorate. Tea Partiers have been angry from the day Obama won the presidential election in November 2008. Not just angry, they have been mad as hell. They protested each and every proposal by Obama that would have helped middle-class and poor Americans. The middle-class and the poor are not stupid, they are not angry with the Obama administration because they know what happened. Rich don't attend rallies. The middle-class and the poor that attended Hillary Clinton's and Bernie Sanders' rallies were not mad with Obama, or the Democratic leadership. In fact they are still quite happy with them.

Democrats are not angry with the Obama administration. Most Republicans are not angry with the Republican Establishment. Democrats and Republicans have never been close buddies. But there has never been any palpable anger between these two groups and they form the vast majority of the electorate. The same goes to the Independents. They align with one party or the other come voting time.

It's the Tea Partiers and a few other Republicans who are angry and they form only a section of the electorate, about thirty five percent (35%) of the Republican voters. They were the Trump supporters during the primary process. Of course, as the election date draws near almost all Republicans will coalesce behind their nominee Trump.

So, let's leave behind the so called "angry electorate' and examine what really went on within the Republican Party during the last eight years.

Split in the Republican Party

In the 2008 presidential election 43% of non-Hispanic Whites voted for Senator Obama. Ordinarily, the 55% non-Hispanic Whites that voted for Senator McCain would have accepted Obama as their president and turned their attention to defeat him at the next presidential election. That is how it's supposed to be unless the newly elected president takes part in some serious misdeeds as President Nixon did or gets assassinated. As to be expected, shortly after the election, leaders of the Republican Party started strategizing to win the white house in 2012. They underestimated the depth of anxiety and horror felt by a section of their voters at the reality of Obama occupying the white house. That was a crucial mistake by the Republican Establishment.

Among the non-Hispanic Whites that didn't vote for Obama, there were some who just couldn't accept an Obama presidency. Why they disliked him so intensely is anybody's guess. Let's not kid ourselves, Obama's race was a factor, but it's hard to believe that it was the only reason. Obama may have appeared too smart and too perfect for them. May be too elite, a social climber, whatever it was these folks just couldn't stand him and didn't want him in the White House. They became the grassroots of the Tea Party movement. They were not concentrated in the so called red states, they were everywhere and social media and private blogs and websites enabled them to connect fast and easy. This was the beginning of the split within the Republican Party.

It was not a division between the RINOS (Republicans in name only) and the Conservatives as some pundits would like to make it out to be. Nor was it a division between Ultra-Conservatives and Conservatives or between Conservatives and Moderate Republicans. It's a safe bet that each and every person with any kind of affiliation with the Republican Party voted for Senator McCain at the 2008 presidential election. It's even a safer bet that those who couldn't stand Obama voted en-masse for Senator McCain not because they cared for McCain but because they didn't want Obama in the White House.

The division within the Republican Party that started after the 2008 presidential election was between those that wouldn't accept Obama as their president even for a day, never mind a full term and those who were content to defeat Obama at the next presidential election in 2012.

The former group gathered with lightning speed to form the Tea party.

The latter group came to be known as the Establishment. The Establishment Republicans include each and every type of Republican other than the Tea Partiers. The notion that Establishment Republicans are not conservative enough is a pure invention. Neo-Conservatives, Ultra- Conservatives, Conservatives, Right to the Center Republicans, Moderate Republicans, they all are among the Establishment Republicans. None among Establishment Republicans liked Obama but they accepted the reality that the only way to get rid of him was to defeat him at the 2012 presidential election or wait for his second term to run out in 2016.

The Establishment Republicans had a choice to make. They could have tried to educate the Tea Partiers of the reality of the situation; (after all Tea Partiers were also Republicans that voted for McCain.) If they considered trying to educate Tea Partiers as a futile exercise, then they could have at least stayed clear of them. But that is not what they did. They embraced the Tea Partiers for short term gain. That was the second crucial mistake by the Establishment Republicans.

The Tea Partiers cared less about the Great Recession or the consequences of their actions. The notion that Tea Party movement was about curtailing government spending, reducing national debt or safeguarding the constitution is a myth. They said they wanted their country back, meaning get Obama out of the White House. That is not to say that some Tea Partiers were not interested in issues of excessive government spending or the national debt or the constitution, but these issues were not the force behind the Tea Party movement. There has never been any movement in recent history centering on any one of these issues or all of them combined. The force behind the Tea Party movement was the burning urge to stop Obama, the guy they couldn't stand. That is the distinction nobody wants to see, talk or write about, may be because it is not politically correct. That is the force that urged ordinary citizens, mostly Republicans to take to the streets to protest each and every proposal by the Obama Administration. The economy was in a Recession, possibly heading in to a Depression and thousands of Tea Partiers were opposing every move by a new Administration to curtail the crisis. It was as if each Tea Partier suddenly became a brilliant economist.

The hostility towards Obama was thinly veiled in the form of protests to the stimulus or whatever else that was proposed by his administration. But the protests would not have galvanized without the backing and support of a few very rich and powerful organizations. *Fox News channel* and *Right-Wing Radio* were prime contributors to publicize the movement. Their vilification of Obama from the day he announced his candidacy was so outlandish that they must have been horrified when the senator won the presidential election. Worse, their audiences needed an explanation and what better remedy than to feed them with more red meat. It didn't look good to personally attack a newly elected black president, but damning his agenda was an excellent alternative.

That is only half the story. Here is the other half.

The Tea Party is only partly responsible for the chaos in the Republican Party. They organized to infiltrate the Republican Party as a part of their plan to stop Obama. Tea Partiers also protested on the streets. It was their right irrespective of how despicable their motives were.

On the other hand, the strategy adopted by the Republican Establishment to regain the White House in 2012 was downright pathetic. Most of these guys were United States senators or members of the House of Representatives. Considering that a new administration was battling what came to be known as the Great Recession, the plan adopted by the Congressional Republicans was unworthy of a major political party.

Republican leaders, conservative think-tanks and right-wing pundits were calling for total obstruction of the new president's agenda. That was even before Obama took the oath of office.

In Robert Draper's book, *Do Not Ask What Good We Do: Inside the U.S. House of Representatives* Draper writes that during a four hour meeting Senior GOP law makers literally plotted to sabotage, undermine and destroy America's economy by saying "No" to everything President Obama proposed.[1] They plotted to bring Congress to a standstill by pledging to obstruct and block President Obama on all legislation.

In his book, Draper describes the sense of unease among Republicans for having lost the White House race the previous November. They were apparently disturbed that 1.8 million were attracted to the mall to witness Obama being sworn in as America's first black president. They were going to do something about it.

On the night of Obama's inauguration fifteen Republicans had gathered at the Caucus Room in Washington, an upscale restaurant where they hatched a plan to make Obama a one term president. Attending the dinner organized by the Republican strategist Frank Luntz, were House members Eric Cantor, Jeb Hensarling, Pete Hoekstra, Dan Lungren, Kevin McCarthy, Paul Ryan and Pete Sessions. From the Senate were Tom Coburn, Bob Corker, Jim DeMint, John Ensign, Jon Kyl. Former House Speaker Newt Gingrich had been the only other attendee. The session lasted four hours and by the end, they had conceived a plan. They would take back the House in November 2010 and use it as a spear to mortally wound Obama in 2011 and take back the Senate and White House in 2012, Draper writes.

Draper quotes Gingrich at the end of the meal: "You will remember this day. You'll remember this as the day the seeds of 2012 were sown."

One wonders? What kind of opposition did we elect in 2008 when our economy was heading to a Depression?

However, with all the protests by the Tea Partiers and obstructions by the Republican Establishment notwithstanding, President Obama was able to advance his agenda during the first two years of his presidency as Democrats controlled both the House and the Senate.

But that changed in 2010.

The Republicans stuck to their plan and the Tea Partiers did their part.

The mid-term congressional election in 2010 was about demonizing Obama. It had little to do with actions taken by the Obama administration to prevent the Great Recession sliding in to a Depression. The Affordable Care Act 2010, Obama Care as it came to be known did play a big part and was made out to be a monster that kills old people. Republicans, with the help of Tea Partiers did an outstanding job of vilifying Obama and were instrumental in handing him a defeat so heavy, that Obama himself called it a shellacking.

Even though the Republicans gained control of the House in 2010 it came with a price. Tea Partiers who helped them wanted their share of the pie. The dangers to the Republican Party were evident during the primary process when Tea Partiers started fielding Tea Party candidates to challenge established Republican candidates. Following are two typical examples:

Tea Partier Christine O'Donnell's defeat of nine-term U.S. Representative Michael Castle in the Senate primary in Delaware ended the career of a Republican moderate in Congress. O'Donnell went on to lose the election in November.

Tea Partier Marco Rubio challenged sitting Florida Governor Charlie Crist in the Senate primary in Florida. The main criticism of Crist was that he accepted Obama's stimulus money for his state. Also that he was too moderate and was too friendly with Obama. Realizing that he was going to lose the primary, Charlie Crist left the Republican Party and fought in the General Election as an Independent. Marco Rubio won the election in November and became the Republican Junior Senator from Florida.

You can see what happened here. Republicans won one senate seat and lost the other. May be if established Republicans were their candidates in both seats they could have won both or perhaps they could have lost both. That however is not what counted in the end. The point was that the Republicans were losing control of their party. When a party loses control of its members it cannot govern and this became evident to Republicans almost immediately after the 2010 mid-term election. In my humble opinion this was the last opportunity for Republicans to distance themselves from the Tea Partiers before their party suffered irreparable damage. They could have done so without losing their majority status in the House, but they didn't. I attribute it to lack of strong leadership.

The bottom line was the Republican Establishment chose to ignore the damage being done to their party and continued to allow Tea partiers to tagalong with them.

In the 2012 presidential election, the Tea Partiers weren't happy with the Republican nominee Gov. Mitt Romney, but they worked their heart out for him not because they loved Romney but because they wanted to defeat Obama. Don't for a moment believe that a single Republican or Tea Partier stayed home or didn't vote for Romney because he wasn't conservative enough. That's a myth invented by political pundits.

Obama didn't just get reelected, he won in a landside. However, Tea Partiers did help Republicans to keep the majority in the House of Representatives. Democrats managed to maintain the majority in the senate but not by much.

Then came the 2014 mid-term elections; and the Tea Partiers not only helped Republicans to keep the House of Representatives with an increased majority, they also helped them get a majority in the senate.

Tea Partiers fought hard for these achievements and wanted to cash in their chips. In their view, they weren't asking for much, they merely wanted Obama and his agenda stopped - instead they find him riding regardless towards the end of his second term. The guy the Tea Partiers never accepted as their president and who has practically ignored them for almost eight years like they never existed is getting ready to leave the White House having done pretty much as he pleased. This has driven the Tea Partiers insane and the Republicans who have failed them are feeling their fury.

They have created so much chaos in the Republican Party that it's time to examine who these Tea Partiers are and how they organized themselves into a party.

The Tea Party

The Tea party is snow white. African-Americans, Hispanics, Asians and other ethnic groups have no place in the Tea Party. It was organized within days of the inauguration of a newly elected black president for the sole purpose of opposing him.

It Started in the Blogosphere

Have you heard of market-ticker.org? [2]. Or the tickerforum.org? [3] That is the blog where the Tea Party started in January 2009. The Market Ticker describes itself as a "Commentary on The Capital Markets" and is run by a man named Karl Denninger. It is in the Market Ticker Forum that a man named Graham Makohoniuk had on January 19, 2009, posted an invitation to "Mail a tea bag to the House of Representatives and Senate" as a protest to the $825 billion stimulus package that the Democratic Party leaders had been putting together to combat the Great Recession. That was the day before the inauguration of Barack Obama as President of the United States.

Also on the same day, January 19, 2009 another Forum member Stephanie Jasky had posted a formal invitation "to a commemorative tea party" suggesting that supporters, in a coordinated effort, send tea bags on February 1, 2009 to Congress.

Next we have Karl Denninger joining the action on the following day, January 20, 2009 the day of inauguration of Barack Obama. Denninger had put up a blog post calling on readers to mail tea bags to the White House and Congress on February 1, 2009 protesting the stimulus.[4]

Following is what was in Karl Denninger's post:

'So long as we have an inauguration drawing this sort of crowd and not a protest about our government blowing $700 billion of our dollars so that The Pigmen *of Wall Street can continue to rob our nation blind, then saddle us with the bill when their bets go bad, we will see no solution.*

I cannot take credit for the idea floated on the forum, but I do like it.

It is time for We The People *to send a strong message to Washington DC - no more. No more loading our children and grandchildren with debt. No more bailing out speculators and bankers who made bets they* knew *were unsafe at the time. No more bailing out people who came to Congress to demand the removal of leverage limits, got what they asked for, then blew themselves up* with the very leverage they demanded to be able to use*.*

No more.

Therefore, on February 1st, which is more than enough time for Barack Obama to be seated in his chair in the West Wing, I am recommending an act of peaceful, lawful and yet unmistakable protest.

That is, to mail President Obama one teabag. Nothing dangerous, nothing illegal - just one teabag.

Send one to your Congressman and one to each Senator.

Later, when the weather is a bit warmer and fountains are running water (rather than frozen!) this sort of protest can be repeated with LOOSE tea in select cities.

But for now, let's start with the symbolism, to be repeated *each and every time our government votes or intends to do something similarly stupid - which I presume will include Obama's "stimulus" package.*

If we all mail our teabags on February 1st, it will send a strong message to Washington. Include a copy of this Ticker, *another Ticker related to the many bailouts (pick one!) or write your own letter condemning the fraud and abuse in our banking and financial system - with the teabag being your symbolic refusal to quietly pay for it.*

Pass it around the blogs and email lists - its a bag of tea folks, and the obvious parallel to the Boston Tea Party of old should be instantly obvious to everyone who receives it.'

- End of Post -

Who were these people so incensed by the proposed stimulus that they started organizing tea bag protests on the day before and on the very day of the inauguration of a new president?

Graham Makohoniuk has been an employee of a company called Globalvest Management Company that was in St. Thomas, Virgin Islands and which had closed in 2007. Prior to that he had been with Export Development Corporation and a Canadian company called The Canada Deposit Insurance Corporation (CDIC).[5]

Then we have Stephanie Jasky with her invitation to a commemorative tea party. A student of Macomb Community College in Greater Detroit Area, Stephanie Jasky has been a paralegal with the law practice of Payne Broder &Fossee, PC. She also has her own website FedUpUSA.org.[6]

Then we have Karl Denninger who wanted tea bags mailed to White House and Congress on February 1st. Mr. Denninger runs his blogs Denninger.net, [7] Market-ticker.org, [2], and Ticker Forum.org. [3] He also contributes to Stephanie Jasky's Fed UPUSA.org. Denninger who had been an accomplished technologist and a businessman in the 1990s had become a financial commentator and trader, and a political activist in the later years. He has been protesting President Bush's efforts to curtail the recession and had continued the trend as Obama took office.

So we have Graham Makohoniuk, Stephanie Jasky and Karl Denninger sharing the honor of making early calls in the blogosphere for Tea Party protests.

Come February 19, 2009, exactly one month from the inauguration of Obama, we have the so called "Santelli' Rant" which some claim gave birth to the Tea Party.

However, before we examine the "Santelli' Rant" we need to visit a few street protests that had been organized prior to the Santelli' Rant.

First Street Protest - Mary Rakovich

The first street protest had been at a town hall meeting on February 10, 2009 held in Fort Myers, Florida and attended by President Obama and Florida Governor Charlie Crist. The purpose of the town hall meeting had been to promote the stimulus package. A woman by the name Mary Rakovich had organized the protest. She and a few others had been holding signs and she had been voicing that the government was wasting too much money and Obama was promoting "Socialism". After the protest, Rakovich had been invited to appear in front of a national audience on Neil Cavuto's Fox News Channel program *Your World* where she has complained about excessive spending policies of the Obama Administration.

Who is Mary Rakovich and what was her protest all about? This woman's protest had been the first street protest against the Obama Administration and had taken place at one of his first town hall meetings since inauguration.

Rakovich is a registered Republican whose first political activity was to volunteer for John McCain's 2008 presidential campaign. At an interview with Edward Luce of FT Magazine Rakovich had admitted that she started to get the feeling that she was losing her country in early 2008 when she heard the incendiary clips "God damn America", "God damn America," in the tapes of Obama's Reverend Jeremiah Wright being played over and over again in the TV networks.[8] That she also heard rumors that Michelle Obama was on tape condemning "whiteys" and that Obama had not been born in America and was a closet Muslim. That she really freaked out when she looked up the website of Reverend Wright's Trinity United Church of Christ and came across black liberation theology.

In an interview with David Montgomery of the Washington Post, Mary Rakovich had admitted that several weeks before her protest, she attended an activist training session held by *Freedom Works*, the Washington-based advocacy group that has supported and promoted the Tea Party movement.[9] Also that the campaign director of Freedom Works, Brendan Steinhauser called her before Obama's visit to Fort Myers, but by that time she and her husband had already decided to try organizing something. When Rakovich appeared in Neil Cavuto's Fox News Channel program *Your World* she had acknowledged that in her activist training session with *Freedom Works* she was taught how to attract more supporters and was specifically advised not to focus on President Obama.

Mary Rakovich has made no mention of a Tea Party in her protest, but is considered by many as a pioneer of the Tea Party movement.

There is no doubt that Freedom Works encouraged her, but what is amazing is the speed with which Fox News Channel moved in to capitalize on the occasion. There had been only few protesters, Mary, her husband and few others and it had been a quiet affair; but it was good enough for Fox News to move in.

Second Street Protest – Keli Carender

First street protest against Obama's stimulus was in Deep South, Fort Myers, Florida. The protest that followed, held on February 16, 2009 was way up North in Seattle, Washington. It was organized by Keli Carender. She had been involved in politics for some time and had played a major role in the 2008 presidential election. Having been the chairwoman of the Washington Young Republicans Federation and the political director of the King County Young Republicans, she had been able to get around 100 people to join the protest. She had her own blog *Redistributing Knowledge* that she was operating under the name "Liberty Belle" where she had posted about the protest.[10] There was no mention of a Tea Party or even the word "Tea" at this protest. Instead it was called a protest against "A Barack Obama Bill Porkulus" which was what the radio talk show host Rush Limbaugh had been calling the stimulus package. According to Michelle Malkin, a conservative blogger who has also helped Carender to publicize the protest, there were about 100 participants at the protest some of whom wore pig noses. Some waved Old Glory and 'Don't Tread on Me' flags.[11] Their handmade signs read 'Obama$ Pokulus$ Wear$ Lip$tick' 'I don't want to pay for the Swindle Us! I am only 10 years old'. At one point a supporter had barged on to the speakers' stage and given a Nazi salute.

Carender's feelings and anger towards Obama are depicted in her own words in one of her statements contained in an article with the heading 'Tea Party Star Leads Movement On Her Own Terms' by Martin Kaste on February 2, 2010 in the NPR Special Series, the Tea Party in America.[12] Her comment has been with reference to the health care reforms. "I tried to boil down in essence what makes me so angry about it," Carender says. "And it was this idea that he and other people decide what the needs are in society. They get to decide. But in order to fund those things, they have to take from some people in order to give to the other people." She refuses to even recognize that Obama has been elected as the president whose job it is to consider what the needs are in society.

Street Protests That Followed

Carender's protest had been followed on the next day February 17, 2009 by a protest in Denver, Colorado organized by the Americans for Prosperity Colorado, the Independence Institute and some others. Called Denver Anti-Stimulus Rally and Pig Roast, it had been organized to coincide with the signing of the stimulus package by President Obama and had been attended by about 200 participants.[13]

The next recorded protest had been in Mesa, Arizona on February 18, 2009 attended by about 500 participants.[14]

We have now arrived at February 18, 2009, one month into the Obama Administration, perhaps a good time to assess where we were.

An economy that had lost millions of jobs in 2008 had lost almost another 600,000 in January 2009. Millions have already lost their homes and millions more were facing foreclosure. You could top that with a full blown financial crisis and two ongoing wars. A new administration was proposing measures to combat the recession and avoid the economy from sliding into a depression.

Blogosphere is buzzing with posts to send tea bags to Congress and White House. Street protests to Obama's stimulus also called porklus as Rush

Limbaugh would have it are being held in states of Florida, Washington, Colorado and Arizona.

This would be a fair and accurate description of the economic and political situation in the country one month into Obama Administration. A few of those Republicans who couldn't accept Obama as their president weren't wasting any time. They had the advantage of the social media and the benefit of simply saying "No" to Obama. The real fireworks started after the so called 'Rick Santelli's rant.'

Rick Santelli's Rant

It's widely believed that an outburst by an on-air-editor which came to be known as the 'Rick Santelli's Rant' gave birth to the Tea Party.

On February 19, 2009 Rick Santelli was an on-air editor, reporting live from the floor of the Chicago Mercantile Exchange for CNBC. The day before, on February 18, 2009, President Obama had announced a $75 billion program, called *The Homeowners Affordability and Stability Plan* to help millions of homeowners facing foreclosure refinance their mortgages. While standing on the floor, Santelli had unleashed what can only be called a rant against this plan. Overall his tirade had been about how President Obama was mismanaging the economy, rewarding "losers," and imperiling the future of freedom. In the midst of his rage, he had called for a new Tea Party.

It is unimaginable as to how quickly the clip was linked to and embedded in so many Conservative websites. A video of his rant went viral on YouTube in a matter of minutes. The reaction to the rant was intense and if you haven't heard or read it before, the following is a transcript: [15]

The Rant

RICK SANTELLI: The government is promoting bad behavior. Because we certainly don't want to put stimulus forth and give people a whopping $8 or $10 in their check, and think that they ought to save it, and in terms of modifications... I'll tell you what, I have an idea.

You know, the new administration's big on computers and technology-- How about this, President and new administration? Why don't you put up a website to have people vote on the Internet as a referendum to see if we really want to subsidize the losers' mortgages; or would we like to at least buy cars and buy houses in foreclosure and give them to people that might have a chance to actually prosper down the road, and reward people that could carry the water instead of drink the water?

TRADER ON FLOOR: That's a novel idea.
(Applause, cheering)

JOE KERNEN: Hey, Rick... Oh, boy. They're like putty in your hands. Did you hear...?

SANTELLI: No they're not, Joe. They're not like putty in our hands. This is America! How many of you people want to pay for your neighbor's mortgage that has an extra bathroom and can't pay their bills? Raise their hand.
(Booing)
President Obama, are you listening?

TRADER: How 'bout we all stop paying our mortgage? It's a moral hazard.
KERNEN: It's like mob rule here. I'm getting scared. I'm glad I'm...
CARL QUINTANILLA: Get some bricks and bats...
SANTELLI: Don't get scared, Joe. They're already

scaring you. You know, Cuba used to have mansions and a relatively decent economy. They moved from the individual to the collective. Now, they're driving '54 Chevys, maybe the last great car to come out of Detroit.

KERNEN: They're driving them on water, too, which is a little strange to watch.

SANTELLI: There you go.

KERNEN: Hey Rick, how about the notion that, Wilbur pointed out, you can go down to 2% on the mortgage...

SANTELLI: You could go down to -2%. They can't afford the house.

KERNEN: ...and still have 40%, and still have 40% not be able to do it. So why are they in the house? Why are we trying to keep them in the house?

SANTELLI: I know Mr. Summers is a great economist, but boy, I'd love the answer to that one.

REBECCA QUICK: Wow. Wilbur, you get people fired up.

SANTELLI: We're thinking of having a Chicago Tea Party in July. All you capitalists that want to show up to Lake Michigan, I'm gonna start organizing.

(Whistling, cheering)

QUICK: What are you dumping in, what are you dumping in this time? Housing...?

SANTELLI: We're going to be dumping in some derivative securities. What do you think about that?

QUINTANILLA: Mayor Daley is marshalling the police right now.

KERNEN: Rabble-rouser.

QUINTANILLA: The National Guard.

After Jason Roney of Sharmac Capital makes some comments, it's back to Santelli.

QUINTANILLA: You know, Rick, one of our producers says if Roland Burris steps down, man, "Senator Santelli," the junior senator from Illinois. It's a possibility. I'm just saying...

SANTELLI: Do you think I want to take a shower every hour? The last place I'm ever gonna live or work is D.C.

KERNEN: Have you raised any money for Blago?

SANTELLI: No, but I think that somebody's gonna have to start raising money for us.

QUICK: Hey, Rick? Can you do that one more time, just get the mob behind you again?

QUINATILLA: Have the camera pull way out.

QUICK: Yeah, pull way out. Everybody listen to Rick Santelli.

KERNEN: He can't... I don't think... You can't just do it at will, can you Rick? I mean, you have to say something.

QUICK: No, do it at will. Let's see.

SANTELLI: Listen, all's I know is, is that there's only about 5% of the floor population here right now, and I talk loud enough they can all hear me. So if you want to ask 'em anything, let me know. These guys are pretty straight forward, and my guess is, a pretty good statistical cross-section of America, the silent majority.

QUICK: Not so silent majority today. So Rick, are they opposed to the housing thing, to the stimulus package, to everything out there?

SANTELLI: You know, they're pretty much of the notion that you can't buy your way into prosperity, and if the multiplier that all of these Washington economists are selling us is over one... that we never have to worry about the economy again. The government should spend a trillion dollars an hour because we'll get 1.5 trillion back.

WILBUR ROSS: Rick, I congratulate you on your new

incarnation as a revolutionary leader.
SANTELLI: Somebody needs one. I'll tell you what, if you read our founding fathers, people like Benjamin Franklin and Jefferson, What we're doing in this country now is making them roll over in their graves.

[Note: Joe Kernen, Carl Quintanilla and Rebecca Quick were all CNBC reporters. Wilbur Ross was an investor]

- End of Transcript -

Well, there you have it. Call it what you may, rant, tirade, screech, outburst or whatever, the above is the episode that apparently released the fury that was burning within those who just couldn't accept Obama as their president far less his administration. Santelli himself has in subsequent interviews called his rant a "match in a dried tinder box".

Following is my take on Santelli's rant:

During his tirade Santelli was promoting a Tea Party rally to be held in July, 2009 with his word: "We're thinking of having a Chicago Tea Party in July. All you Capitalists that want to show up to Lake Michigan, I'm gonna start organizing."

This discredits his subsequent assertions that his rant was impromptu. During the preceding month the blogosphere has been buzzing with calls to mail tea bags to the White House and Congress, it started in the Market-Ticker forum the day before Obama was inaugurated. His words leave no doubt that he had been planning with some others to hold a Tea party in Chicago sometime in July and was making use of his position as an on-air reporter to get the message out. What I don't understand, though, is why he subsequently claimed it to be spontaneous; we live in a free country, he said what he had to say and he had every right and freedom to do so. It is possible that he himself knew what he was doing was not kosher. His was a calling to stop helping millions of house owners who were trying to avoid foreclosure and stay in their homes.

Santelli also used insulting and derogatory language to describe the homeowners who were having trouble paying their mortgages. He called them "losers," "those who drink the water instead of carry the water," "your neighbors who have an extra bathroom and can't pay their bills." This is strong language that is not expected of an on air floor reporter of CNBC. On the one hand his rant incites those who oppose Obama and on the other, it humiliates the already hurting homeowners. With humiliation comes anger. In this type of circumstance the fury is always directed at the government of the day. I have to believe that Santelli knew exactly what he was doing when attacking these homeowners.

Santelli was also directly challenging Obama; a newly elected president, very popular at the time, just one month in to his administration, not the kind of stuff that someone in Santelli's position would do without giving considerable thought. Not only was he challenging Obama, he was also insinuating that Obama's one month old administration was heading towards Communism. Note his words: "You know, Cuba used to have mansions and a relatively decent economy. They moved from the individual to the collective. Now, they're driving '54 Chevys, maybe the last great car to come out of Detroit."

Then he refers to the traders on the floor who had been cheering and booing as *the silent majority,* an obvious reference to President Nixon's era.

Santeli had received both admiration and criticism for his rant. The following is an example:

An article by Eric Etheridge on February 20, 2009 in the Opinion pages of the New York Times titled *Rick Santelli: Tea Party Time,* refers to writings by Kathryn Jean Lopez and Larry Kudlow both at National Review Online supporting Santelli, and writings by Charles Lemos at MyDD and John Cole at Balloon Juice opposing him.[16]

Following are excerpts of relevant sections of Etheridge's article:

Yesterday Rick Santelli, who reports from the floor of the Chicago Board of Trade for CNBC, unleashed a rant against Obama's newly announced housing bailout plan, intended to help some homeowners refinance mortgages and avoid foreclosure. The clip was quickly linked to and embedded in Web sites everywhere, and provoked intense reaction that pretty much broke along partisan lines.

At National Review Online, for example, Kathryn Jean Lopez was busting out the Palin-Santelli 2012 posters:

"I've had a case of deja vu today. I'm noticing the tone. I'm seeing the enthusiasm. And I'm digging out from the sheer volume of e-mails I've been getting today about that CNBC dude. The reaction to Rick Santelli's Chicago-trading-floor incident this morning

echoes the emotional reaction my inbox had to Sarah Palin's convention speech this summer.

I make no endorsements. It's just an observation.

I think people are hungry for someone who is fed up with the way things are and who seem to believe in something enough to know there in an alternative worth fighting for. Some of the voices may be far from perfect, but Americans are looking for signs of the life of an alternative. And so if a representative pops up — someone who appears to have roots and energy, folks will cheer them on in the hopes there's a candidate here. Maybe not a presidential candidate, but a leader of some sort. Someone who can offer a vision of something other than a culture of bailout.

Today, Rick Santelli was that sign of life".

Also at NRO, Larry Kudlow seconded Santelli's call for a Chicago Tea Party to protest the housing plan:

"Team Obama is rewarding bad behavior. It is enlarging moral hazard. It is expanding its welfarist approach to economic policy. And with a huge expansion of government-owned zombie lenders Fannie Mae and Freddie Mac, Team Obama is taking a giant step toward nationalizing the mortgage market. . .

Reporting from the Chicago commodity pits, my CNBC colleague Rick Santelli unleashed a torrent of criticism against this scheme. Santelli said: "Government is promoting bad behavior. . . . Do we really want to subsidize the losers' mortgages? This is America! How many of you people want to pay for your neighbor's mortgage? President Obama, are you listening? How about we all stop paying our mortgages! It's a moral hazard." All this took place on the air, to the cheers of traders. Santelli called for a new tea party in support of capitalism. He's right."

At My DD, Charles Lemos weighed in with his experience of Wall Street:

"After watching the [Santelli clip], I first had to check my calendar. Somehow I felt I traveled back in time to the early 1970s to witness first hand Richard Nixon's "northern strategy," his pursuit of white ethnic voters who were so deeply disaffected over Great Society programs ranging from desegregation (remember the Boston busing madness?) to affirmative action among others that they would desert the Democratic Party becoming "Nixon's silent majority" and "Reagan Democrats". . . .

Rick Santelli is heir to this legacy laced with racist overtones. Note the promo before the rant in the video link at CNBC. CNBC has an upcoming special entitled The Rise of America's New Black Overclass. Fear mongering, it's worked before so let's try it again. It's back to the 1970s for the GOP and their rabid white ethnics.

I spent a decade on Wall Street working for Alex. Brown & Sons, Deutsche Banc Securities and Goldman Sachs. I found Wall Street a largely liberal environment with one major exception, the trading floor. In my experience I found traders, who are largely white ethnics — Irish, Italian, Greek, Polish or Slovak among others — and graduates of the Seton Halls, the Boston Colleges, the Notre Dames, the

Penn States were the most rabid conservative and foul mouthed people on the planet. Nor could any of them ever get my name right. "My name is Charles, not Chuckie" was something I would repeat whenever I had the misfortune to have to interact with them. Some of these folks made William Buckley appear moderate."

At Balloon Juice, John Cole marveled at Santelli's "audacity":

"The most amusing thing to me about this Rick Santelli faux populist broker revolt is not his invocation of the Nixonian silent majority, but the utter lack of perspective it displays. Yes, there is a simmering discontent and anger out there, and clearly the Republicans are going to try to tap into it, but the problem for Santelli and his crowd is that the anger is not directed at the people who are losing their homes, but at the people Santelli spends every day rubbing shoulders with at the trendy Chicago restaurants the brokers go to these days.

The audacity of Santelli's "revolt" is that a mere 75 billion is being spent to help struggling families repackage loans- a mere pittance in the terms of the gargantuan amount of money being thrown at the banks, the Wall Street wizards, and the rest of the rocket scientists who are the root of this problem".

- End of Excerpts -

There were many others that supported and opposed Santanlli. The bottom line, though, is that his rant was good enough to unleash the Tea Party Movement.

The Rapid Rise of the Tea Party

The response to Rick santelli's call for a new Tea Party was instant. What followed can only be described as a major operation, implemented with urgency. The following account is based on information in an article in Wikipedia the free encyclopedia under the main title "Tea Party Protests" and sub-heading: 'Birth of the National Tea Party Movement'.[17] The article contains a pretty decent account of how rapidly the movement advanced following Santelli's Rant:

The day following Santelli's comments from the Chicago Mercantile Exchange, roughly 50 national Conservative leaders participated in a conference call that gave birth to the national Tea Party movement. In response to Santelli, websites such as ChicagoTeaParty.com, registered in August 2008 by Chicago radio producer Zack Christenson, were live within twelve hours. About 10 hours after Santelli's remarks, reTeaParty.com was bought to coordinate Tea Parties scheduled for the 4th of July and within two weeks was reported to be receiving 11,000 visitors a day.

Also on February 19, Young Americans for Liberty NY State Chairman Trevor Leach created a Facebook page called "The Capitalist Chicago Tea Party— Rick's Revolution", in response to Santelli's call for a national Tea Party. According to The Huffington Post, a Facebook page was developed on February 20 calling for Tea Party protests across the country. Eric Odom of the Conservative activist group Freedom Works was one of the group administrators, and it was created by Phil Kerpen from the Conservative advocacy organization, Americans for Prosperity.

Soon, the "Nationwide Chicago Tea Party" protests were coordinated across over 40 different cities for February 27, 2009, establishing the first national modern Tea Party protest.

That is how rapidly the movement propagated – It only took five weeks from Obama's inauguration for a nationwide protest against his agenda to be organized.

The why and the how of the beginning and growth of the Tea party are not hard to understand as long as you ask the right question and are willing to accept the obvious answers.

Why were so many Americans not willing to give Obama some time, any time, even a few months to implement his policies and turn the economy around? After all he was elected in a landslide to clear a mess that was not his doing. There are many obvious answers: they didn't trust Obama; they didn't like the guy; they didn't want to have anything to do with Obama because he was black; they didn't want Obama to be successful as radio talk host Rush Limbaugh declared over the air waves and I would add one more, that they didn't want him in the White House. It didn't look good for grass-root Tea Partiers to admit how they really felt about Obama. So they put forward their twisted and warped economic theories to explain why Obama had to be stopped, stopped before he could even start. It was as if these guys and gals on the street were all maestro economists. But the cat did get out of the bag often enough in their rallies. The hatred to the man was too much to be suppressed all the time. So we saw the posters in the Tea Party rallies depicting Obama as a monkey, as a witch doctor, as a racist, a Nazi and so many other caricatures with racial undertones.

Even with all the freely available avenues in the social media, the Tea Party movement couldn't have reached such heights without the help of some rich and powerful organizations.

Fox News played a major role in promoting the Tea Party. Glen Beck was with CNN Headline News when Obama was a candidate for president but had joined Fox News in January 2009. The contribution by him and Sean Hannity to publicize the Tea Party movement was huge.

Freedom Works, an advocacy group headed by former Republican House majority leader Dick Armey played a key role in the Tea Party movement from the very start.[18] So did The Americans for Prosperity Foundation chaired by billionaire David Koch.[19]

Sen. Jim DeMint of South Carolina supported Tea Party candidates from within the Republican establishment.[20]

The Tea Party wouldn't have been half as effective if not for the constant support by the Rightwing Talk Radio. Their support was unconditional. The theme was sharp and easy to follow: Obama was a danger to the United States, he was Un-American, he was not even born in the United States and was not qualified to be president, his was an illegitimate administration, the guy cannot be trusted, he was a closet Muslim pretending to be a Christian, he was only helping blacks, he hated whites, Tea Party will take the country back from this communist monster, and it went on and on twenty four-seven. It started in the early morning hours with William (Bill) Bennet who used to be the Secretary of Education under Ronald Regan and a "drug czar" under George Bush. Rush Limbaugh, Glen Beck, Sean Hannity, Michael Savage and Mark Levin were just a few of the prominent radio talk hosts that supported the Tea Party and went after Obama mercilessly. It was brutal.

The chickens have come home to roost

Republican Party was not in the best of shape at the end of President George W. Bush's second term in 2008. There were many reasons and they were all based on policy. A majority of the electorate that initially supported Bush policies on domestic affairs and his war policies turned against the Republicans in 2008 and they lost not only the presidency, but also the House and the Senate.

During George W. Bush's two terms, the Democrats objected to most of his policies but stood firmly with him when 9-11 happened. They particularly objected to his tax policies and the Iraq war but there was never a question that they deliberately tried to sabotage the economy for political gain.

Unfortunately, the same cannot be said of the Republicans' conduct during the seven years and five months so far under President Obama. Even before Barack Obama was inaugurated as president, Republican leaders, conservative think-tanks and right wing- pundits were calling for total obstruction of the new president's agenda. Their leaders in Congress plotted to obstruct everything Obama proposed to make his presidency a failure with no regard to how it would negatively affect the economy and thereby the American people. When Tea Partiers got elected to Congress in 2010, they put the Republican policy of obstruction on steroids.

First it was the campaign against the stimulus package, a measure introduced to curtail the Great Recession and avoid the nation sliding into a Depression. Then it was against efforts to combat the housing crisis. Thereafter were the protests against measures to stabilize the Financial Sector and the American Automobile Industry.

Objections to the expansion of the State Children's Health Insurance Program (S-CHIP) to four million more American kids was a clear sign of how desperate Tea Partiers and Republicans were to prevent Obama from getting anything done.

The Affordable Care Act made them totally insane. It was an effort to improve a badly broken health care system. But that didn't matter. They started calling it 'Obamacare' not as a compliment but as a derogatory term. Republicans with Tea Party backing tried everything they possibly could to prevent health care legislation being passed in Congress. When that failed they attempted repeatedly to repeal the Health Care Act or some part of it which would make it ineffective. At the last count there were 51 such attempts.

The Republicans and the Tea Partiers even shutdown the federal government from **October 1 through 16, 2013 in an effort to delay the Affordable Care Act.**

Then they brought the United States to the brink of default over their refusal to increase the nation's debt ceiling which resulted in downgrading of the U.S. credit rating.

Their opposition to a bill that would extend unemployment benefits to 2.5 million jobless Americans was not only cruel but damaging to the economy.

They prevented the American Jobs Act from passing which according to independent analysts could have created as many as two million jobs in 2012. It was an Act that was fully paid for.

They filibustered in the Senate an infrastructure bill, a measure to promote job growth by providing $60 billion to fund transportation projects and create a new infrastructure bank.

They filibustered in the Senate a bipartisan Transportation and Housing Bill that would have invested in infrastructure and housing projects.

Republican senators and Tea Partiers blocked a Democrat-led effort to raise the federal minimum wage to $10.10 an hour.

It is estimated that there are over eleven million undocumented immigrants living in the United States. They have been here for many years and most of the adults have been working without paying any federal or state taxes as they do not have any legal papers. They also have been unable to contribute to any type of medical insurance. Studies also show that given some sort of legal status, some of them would start their own businesses which would be a tremendous boost to the economy. Even most Republicans have been in favor of addressing this issue but the Tea Partiers and some Republicans have successfully obstructed every effort by the Obama administration in finding a suitable resolution to this problem.

Republicans and the Tea Partiers did their absolute best to prevent the Obama administration from finding a peaceful resolution to the nuclear issue with Iran. The pressure they brought on Obama was intense. It included an invitation to Israel Prime Minister **Benjamin Netanyahu to address a joint session of congress on the dangers of a nuclear deal with Iran.**

And so the list goes on of deliberate actions and inactions by the congressional Tea Partiers and Republicans to prevent progress being made under Obama Administration. It was always at the cost of the middle class and the poor.

Republicans won big in the 2010 mid-term elections and gained control of the House of Representatives. They did so with the help of the Tea Party. They retained their majority in the House in the 2012 presidential election and again in the mid-terms in 2014. They also gained control of the Senate in 2014 mid-terms.

Cardinal rule of governance is that when you are in the majority in the House or the Senate or in both, the voters who gave you that majority expect you to govern. Republicans under pressure from the Tea partiers threw this rule out the window. Their singular purpose was to prevent President Obama for getting anything constructive done.

For over five long years of his administration President Obama tried his best to work with the Republicans in Congress. It was to no avail for the obvious reason that it was against the more or less openly disclosed policy of the Republicans. They simply didn't want Obama to be successful, and cooperating with him was not in the Republican agenda. Some Republicans must have known that this policy of theirs will have repercussions, as it was directly hurting the middle class and the poor. It was nearly impossible to grow an economy with this type of obstruction from Republicans who had a majority in the House and the Senate.

Finally in 2014 President Obama started to pointedly criticize Republicans that their policy of obstruction is keeping the system rigged for those at the top, and rigged against the middle class. He addressed the issue in one of his weekly addresses in June 2014: "The problem is, Republicans in Congress keep blocking or voting down almost every serious idea to strengthen the middle class. We could do so much more as a country – as a strong, tight-knit family – if Republicans in Congress were less interested in stacking the deck for those at the top, and more interested in growing the economy for everybody." "They don't do anything except block me and call me names," he added.[21]

2014 was also the year that that President Obama, fed up with Republican obstructionism said at a cabinet meeting on January 14: "We're not just going to be waiting for legislation in order to make sure that we're providing Americans the kind of help they need. I've got a pen and I've got a phone,"[21]

True to his words, on some issues vital to the national interest and where Congress refused to act, President Obama issued executive orders that would achieve the desired result. The Republicans' response was to challenge these executive orders in court and stall them as much as possible. In as much as Republicans had every right to make these challenges the general public was gradually getting wise to what they were doing.

Democrats did a very poor job of making it known to the public what exactly the Republicans were up to. Fortunately, though, the vast majority of Americans have been wise enough to look in to and discover what the Republicans were doing. However, they did take their time to do so. Important measures did get done during the first two years of Obama Administration when the Democrats were in the majority in the House and the Senate. When the Republicans won the House in 2010, their strategy was to bring all progress to a standstill. What they were doing was so cynical that it is surprising that Americans were not quick to be wise to it. Around the beginning of 2015, they finally did and for the Republican establishment *'the chickens have come home to roost'.*

That's when the chaos in the GOP started. The Republican voters started questioning their leaders (Republican establishment) as to why the wages are stagnant for the middle class. Why is it that some major companies are moving their manufacturing to foreign lands and exporting good paying jobs. The Republican standard reply 'Blame Obama for high taxes and too much regulation' isn't cutting any ice any more. Their voters know that the rich pay very little taxes by making use of the loopholes in the tax code that their leaders have so diligently safeguarded. They also have realized that it's the lack of regulations that brought about the financial crisis and that in spite of Dodd-Frank regulations Wall Street is booming.

The frustration of the Tea party grassroots is far worse. They could care less of the economy or the conservative principles, they wanted Obama stopped. They worked their hearts out for the Republicans and won them the House in 2010 and the Senate in 2014 to stop Obama. What happened? From their point of view, the guy they hated, and who has treated them as if they never existed, is happily marching towards the end of his second term having done pretty much as he pleased. This makes them insane and the fury is directed at the Republican establishment.

And what did some average Republican voters and grass-root Tea Partiers do? They found a new leader, the businessman from New York, Donald J. Trump. He is a perfect fit for the Tea Partiers. He is the guy who challenged Obama's right to even hold office as president. Trump didn't let it go after Obama was elected in 2008, he led the birther movement for years and forced Obama to produce his long form birth certificate. This type of stuff has never been associated with the American presidency before. Tea Partiers loved Trump for that.

Trump also became a hero to some (not all) average Republicans and Conservatives who are not Tea Partiers. They are mostly either middle class or poor. You will be surprised to find that there are a whole lot of very poor Republicans and Conservatives. They have had enough of their established leaders: the senators, the House reps., and the governors. They believe these leaders have let them down and quite rightly so. They were looking for somebody different and found Trump. Different, Trump certainly is.

CHAPTER – 4

Why Not Donald Trump

Businessman from New York, Donald J. Trump is the nominee of the Republican Party for President of the United States in the 2016 presidential election. He went through the primary process in full compliance with the Republican Party rules and won the nomination fare and square.

It's perhaps also accurate to say that a bombastic Trump mocked his way to victory. He demolished his fellow candidates with nothing but crude personal insults. It was a most unusual primary.

There have been reservations on the part of some Establishment Republicans and Conservatives to Trump's candidacy, but the likelihood is that the party will coalesce behind him as the election approaches.

Who is Donald Trump

Donald Trump was born on June 14, 1946 in Queens, New York. He was the fourth child of Mary Anne and Fred Trump. Fred Trump was a wealthy real estate owner and businessman. You could say Donald was born rich.

He has three siblings, sisters Maryanne and Elizabeth, both elder to him and Robert, a younger brother. Fred, an elder brother had passed away. Maryanne is a federal judge.

Trump had been married three times and now lives with his third wife Melania. His former spouses were Ivana Trump and Marla Maples.

He has five children: Donald Trump Jr., Ivanka and Eric with his first wife Ivana Trump. Tiffany is his only child with his second wife Marla Maples. His youngest, Barron is his only child with his current wife Melania.

Trump attended Fordham University in Bronx for two years and entered Wharton School of Business at the University of Pennsylvania and graduated from Wharton in 1988.

Mr. Trump is a wealthy businessman and his big claim to readiness for the presidency is his business record. Hence, a thorough scrutiny of his business ventures is fair game. However, Trump's rivals in the Republican primary or the news organizations that were covering his campaign weren't interested. This is surprising because throughout the primary process Trump boasted of his wealth and his skills as a businessman, a builder and a dealmaker. Perhaps, his rivals were too shocked by the nasty insults thrown at them. As for the news media, Trump gave them so much material with his attacks on minorities, his fellow candidates, and on media itself that it may be they didn't feel the need to dig in to his business record.

Trump ridiculed other candidates for fundraising and having "super-packs." He relished boasting that he was self-financing his campaign unlike the others who would be in the pockets of their donors. He particularly went after Governor Bush and his super-pack for the $100M raised.

There has been no shortage of allegations against Trump's business practices. His now discontinued Trump University has been accused of fraud, unfair business practices and false advertising.

There have been accusations from people who have worked for Trump that they have not been paid properly. Likewise there have been similar accusations from contractors, and vendors of his projects. There have been lawsuits filed against Trump and or his organizations on these issues.

Trump's Taj Mahal casino, The Trump Plaza Hotel and Trump Entertainment Resorts had all filed for bankruptcy at one stage or the other.

Now that we have entered the general election phase, one hopes that there would be a proper scrutiny of Trump's business career. His tax-returns would have been helpful but trump hasn't released them so far. Initially he said his returns are being audited and he will release them when the audit is completed. Subsequently, he has said that he has no plans to release them before the November election, that there's nothing to learn from them and that in any event it is nobody's business. For several decades presidential candidates have released their tax returns for public scrutiny but Trump seems unfazed by that.

So, we are reduced to rely on information available in the public domain to get some idea of Mr. Trump's business career and wealth.

International Business Degree Guide provides following lists of Mr. Trump's business ventures and his wealth [1]

Successful Business Ventures

Grand Hyatt Hotel (1974-)
Wollman Rink (1986-)
Trump Palace (1974-)
Trump Tower (1980-)
40 Wall Street (1995-)
Trump International Tower Chicago (2005-)
Trump Model Management (1999-)
The Apprentice (2004-) NBC cut ties with trump in 2015

Failed Business Ventures

Trump Vodka (2006-2011)
Trump The Game (1989-1990); (2005)
Trump Airlines (1988-1992)
Trump Entertainment Resorts – Casino entity (1995-2015)
GoTrump.com (2006-2007)
Trump Magazine (2007-2008)
Trump Steaks (2007-2012? Unsure when company bowed - possibly 2012)
Trump University (2005-2011)
Trump Ice (1995-2010)
Trump Mortgage (2006-2007)
New Jersey Generals (1983-1985)

How much is Trump really worth?

International Business Degree Guide provides the
following values according to the respective sources:
Trump: over $10B
Forbes: $4B
Bloomberg: 2.9B
North Fork bank (2005): $1.2B
Wall Street Journal: over $1.5B
Deutsche Bank: $788MM
New York Times (2005): $150-$250MM

Above information gives credit to Mr. Trump's claim
that he is a wealthy man, albeit, by not as much as he
claims to be. It's also clear that he has been in
business for a long time with both successful and
failed ventures.

So, we have a wealthy businessman in Trump with
questionable business practices. Let's examine to
what extent his wealth and business experience is
relevant to his quest for the presidency.

What do Americans look for in a President

The President is the head of state and head of
government of the United States. He leads the
executive branch of the federal government and is the
commander-in-chief of the United States Armed
Forces. He is also the Guardian of the Economy. The
United States has the strongest military in the world
and the largest economy. Accordingly, the presidency
of the United States is considered the most powerful
office in the world.

Every four years Americans have the responsibility to elect a man or woman worthy to occupy this powerful office. We have learned from the past that there is no room for error. Electing a person unworthy will have disastrous consequences not only for the United States of America but also for the entire world.

So, what do American voters look for in a president?

NBC News/Wall Street Journal pollsters have conducted a poll in April 2015 to find what the voters want – and don't want - in a presidential candidate.[2]

Pollsters have asked whether specific candidate traits would make a respondent "enthusiastic," "comfortable," "have reservations" or "uncomfortable." By subtracting the positive responses from the negative ones, they have got a pretty good picture of what the most acceptable and unacceptable traits might be for a presidential candidate.

Following are the results:

General Election Voters

% who are enthusiastic/comfortable MINUS % who have reservations/are uncomfortable

An African-American – Positive 75%
A woman – Positive 74%
A person under the age of 50 – Positive 66%
A Hispanic – Positive 63%
Someone with a military background – Positive 62%
A governor – Positive 62%
A Catholic – Positive 57%
A person running as an Independent – Positive 49%

A person who is gay or lesbian – Positive 33%
A U.S. senator – Positive 31%
Has a former president in their family – Positive 27%
A person over 65 – Positive 23%
A first term senator – Positive 7%
An evangelical Christian – Positive 7%
No college degree – Negative 22%
A leader of the Tea Party movement – Negative 28%
No previous elected experience – Negative 39%

Democratic Primary Voters

% who are enthusiastic/comfortable MINUS % who have reservations/are uncomfortable

A woman – Positive 90%
An African-American – Positive 85%
A person under the age of 50 – Positive 74%
A Hispanic – Positive 74%
Someone with a military background – Positive 57%
A person who is gay or lesbian – Positive 55%
A U.S. senator – Positive 55%
A Catholic – Positive 48%
Has a former president in their family – Positive 46%
A governor – Positive 45%
A person running as an Independent – Positive 35%
A person over 65 – Positive 25%
A first term senator – Positive 20%
An evangelical Christian – Negative 29%
No college degree – Negative 50%
No previous elected experience – Negative 55%
A leader of the Tea Party movement – Negative 78%

Republican Primary Voters

% who are enthusiastic/comfortable MINUS % who have reservations/are uncomfortable

Someone with a military background – Positive 90%
A Catholic – Positive 79%
A governor – Positive 74%
A person under the age of 50 – Positive 73%
A Hispanic – Positive 69%
An African-American – Positive 66%
A U.S. senator – Positive 55%
A woman – Positive 54%
An evangelical Christian – Positive 52%
A person over 65 – Positive 45%
Has a former president in their family – Positive 41%
A leader of the Tea Party movement – Positive 25%
A person running as an Independent – Positive 25%
A first term senator – Negative 2%
No college degree – Negative 13%
A person who is gay or lesbian – Negative 15%
No previous elected experience – Negative 16%

The above poll was taken in April 2015 as Democrats and Republicans were preparing for the 2016 primaries. Prospective candidates of both parties have either already made or were making exploratory committees. Fourteen months later they have their nominees.

Democrats settled on a candidate well in line with the preferences indicated in the poll of the Democratic primary voters. A 'woman' was leading their list of positive preferences and they settled on Hillary. Also

Hillary doesn't fall into any of their negative categories.

Democrats had a primary based mostly on policy. Media tried to make out that the close contest between Secretary Hillary Clinton and Senator Bernie Sanders was evidence that Hillary was a weak candidate. Republicans mocked Hillary that she could hardly put away a socialist. This is nonsense. Democrats have always had hotly contested primaries based on policy issues, the most recent being between Hillary Clinton and Barack Obama. The hottest issue at the time was the Iraq war.

Republicans on the other hand did the exact opposite of what Democrats did in selecting their candidate. They selected Donald Trump. He fits in to the category with the highest negatives in their preference list – "No previous elected experience." He doesn't fit in to a single positive category.

Why did Republican voters settle on a candidate who is the exact opposite of the type of person they said they preferred at the start of the primary process? The previous chapter, *Chaos in the GOP* sets out in detail how the Tea party and the Republicans made fertile ground for someone like Trump to emerge.

Trump's past flirtations with White House bids

Donald Trump has had an eye for the presidency for quite some time.

In 1987 there was a move to draft him as a Republican Party candidate but Trump maintained he didn't envision running in 1988.

In 1999, he quit the Republican Party and formed an exploratory committee to help him decide whether to run for president in 2000 as a Reform Party candidate.[3] A few months later he opted against a campaign, excuse being he is convinced the Reform Party candidate couldn't win.

There were reports that Trump was considering presidential runs in 2004 and 2008 but no campaigns materialized.

There were definite hints that he was considering a run in 2012 and it was in the previous year that he started questioning President Obama's citizenship. Yet again though, he decided against running stating business is his greatest passion.

Preparing ground for 2016

Trump launched a public pursuit of Obama's birth certificate in 2011, announcing that he has sent private investigators to Hawaii to see what they could find. Trump clearly knew this was a bogus claim but was pursuing it anyway. He didn't like his chances in 2012 and was obviously preparing for a 2016 presidential run. He continued pushing the 'birther issue. One may wonder why? Even though Obama will not be running in 2016, he knew how much the Tea Partiers and some Conservatives hated the president. They were furious when Obama was reelected in 2012. The fault for the loss they placed squarely on Establishment Republicans.

Tea Partiers and these Conservatives were easy picks and trumped wasted no time. He appealed to them by questioning over and over, whether or not Barack Obama was actually born in the United States. This was music to Obama haters' ears. Trump was building a constituency, a faithful base. Trump pushed it hard enough that Obama in 2014 released his long-form birth certificate to prove that he was born in Hawaii. Can you imagine how far Trump has pursued the birther movement that a sitting president elected for a second term had to release his long-form birth certificate to prove that he could legally hold office? However, Trump didn't stop questioning the president's birth place even after the release of the long-form birth certificate. On the contrary he doubled down, and in addition also wanted to see Obama's college records. Fox News channel and right-wing talk-radio went along with Trump in pushing the birther issue, perhaps ignorant of what trump was up to. Little surprise when you consider their unmitigated opposition to Obama. At one point Trump offered five million dollars which he increased to fifty million dollars to see the president's college records.

By the time Trump announced his candidacy in June 2015 he had a solid voter-base, the Obama haters who easily formed a good twenty five to thirty percent of Republican primary voters. While Trump was solidifying a voter-base, his fellow candidates, there were sixteen of them, were fund raising. For example, former Governor Jeb Bush and his super-pack had one hundred million dollars but hardly any voters. Republican primary voters who were not with

Trump were hopelessly divided among all the other candidates.

I have a few questions. What type of man would initiate his presidential campaign on a despicable lie that the first black president is illegitimate? How vicious and racist is that? Would you trust him with all the powers of the office of president? I wouldn't.

Trump announces his 2016 Campaign

Trump announced his candidacy for president on June 16, 2015 on the theme "make America great again"! Codeword "Black Obama ruined America. I'll make it great again." This was an immediate hit with Obama haters.

Trump's campaign announcement speech was extra ordinary. [4] He attacked some of his fellow candidates and then went after President Obama and Hillary Clinton. He chastised immigrants and called Mexicans drug dealers, criminals and rapists. Many political pundits and Republican candidates ridiculed it at their own risk. Trump knew exactly what he was doing. It was a well thought out and superbly crafted speech to feed his base, the base he had carefully nurtured with the birther issue. He followed it up with blatant personal attacks on fellow candidates. It worked like magic. Within three to four weeks he was polling twenty five to thirty percent of the Republican primary voters. Political pundits and Trump's fellow candidates were puzzled. They were either deliberately refusing to acknowledge or too dumb to realize what Trump had done. Their reasoning was the so called 'angry electorate.'

Name Recognition

Trump also had a tremendous advantage when it came to name recognition. There were governors and United States Senators among his primary contenders, but Trump was better known than any of them. Several factors contributed to his nationwide name recognition.

To start with, Trump became well known in the American financial scene as a real estate magnate.

Over the years Trump has authored several books, but the one that got him really famous was "The Art of the Deal" in 1987.

Trump's first marriage to Ivana, a model, the divorce and the second marriage to Marla Maples, a beauty queen and model were tabloid stuff. And so was his divorce from Marla Maples and the third marriage to yet another model Melania.

He got bad publicity for the bankruptcies involving his casinos.

Trump more or less became a household name with his TV realty show *The Apprentice* which was a huge hit and ran for over a decade.

His flirtations with running for president and the birther movement against President Obama made him famous among some and notorious among others.

Bottom line, when he announced his candidacy for real in June 2015, The Donald was a well known figure with a solid voter base.

GOP Primary

Seventeen Republicans sought their party nomination for president.

Among them were three sitting governors: John Kasich, Scott Walker and Chris Christie and six former governors: Jeb Bush, Jim Gilmore, Rick Perry, Bobby Jindal, George Pataki and Mike Huckabee.

There were four sitting U.S. senators: Ted Cruz, Marco Rubio, Lindsey Graham and Rand Paul and one former U.S. senator Rick Santorum.

Retired neurosurgeon Ben Carson, and former CEO of Hewlett-Packard Carley Fiorina were respectively the only African American and female candidates.

And of course there was Donald Trump, the businessman from New York.

Sixteen of the seventeen candidates began running customary GOP primary campaigns. They were mostly concerned with raising funds. Jeb Bush and his super-packs have already amassed a cool one hundred million dollars. Rumor had it that Scott Walker was the preferred candidate of the billionaire Koch brothers. Each candidate was trying to outdo the other on being the strongest conservative. General consensus was that vicious attacks on President Obama were mandatory to have any chance at winning the primary. Little they knew that another candidate already had the Obama haters nicely lined up behind him.

Donald Trump had different ideas of how to run a primary campaign to win the Republican Party nomination. He already had built for himself a solid voter-base, the Obama haters. His strategy was simple: attack, attack and attack. Shock and awe the opposition by devastating personal attacks. Attack somebody when policy issues are brought up. Deflect is the operative word. Policy is not his thing. Continue to attack President Obama and start on Hillary Clinton. It was an easy plan to implement. In his world attacks didn't have to be based on fact. Hardly any research was necessary. Just make it up as you go. It worked like a dream.

Personal attacks on fellow GOP candidates

Poor Rick Perry, a former governor of the second largest state in the Union, Texas, was one of Trump's early victims. Perry announced his candidacy at a rally in a hangar on Addison Airport, near Dallas. There were reports that the air conditioning in the hangar didn't work properly and it was uncomfortable inside and also that the hanger was too large for the crowd. Trump made use of this circumstance to mock, insult and ridicule Perry. A few weeks later while making his announcement speech Trump referred to this incident as follows:

"And, I can tell, some of the candidates, they went in. They didn't know the air-conditioner didn't work. They sweated like dogs. They didn't know the room was too big, because they didn't have anybody there. How are they going to beat ISIS? I don't think it's gonna happen." [4]

Trump basically compared Perry and his supporters to sweating dogs and this was with no provocation at all on Perry's part. Trump and Perry have been at least acquaintances if not friends. Subsequently Perry did go after Trump, at one point saying that the businessman was becoming a "cancer" to conservatism. They kept up a public feud to almost the day Perry suspended his campaign. A good example: Perry suggesting that "Trump-ism" involves a toxic mix of demagoguery and nonsense," after which Trump saying Perry "should be forced to take an IQ test" before the first GOP debate. It was nasty and ugly.

Trump went after former Florida Governor Jeb Bush with a vengeance. Jeb's father is former president George H.W. Bush. Former president George W. Bush is his brother. Jeb and his super-pack had put together a cool One Million Dollars by the time Trump entered the race. Trump must have seen Jeb, with these advantages, as his main rival. Jeb on the other hand didn't appear to consider Trump as a serious candidate. That was a recipe for disaster. What were Jeb's advisors thinking?

Trump belittled, insulted, mocked and laughed at Jeb from the get go. "Low energy" was Trumps assigned name for Jeb. It stuck because Jeb is a reserved type of guy, a gentleman, and it got under Jeb's skin. Things got extreme in the Republican presidential debate on February 13, 2016 in South Carolina. I was watching it at my home on TV and often with my mouth hanging open. Trump spent much of the evening mocking Jeb as a no-energy, incompetent, lying loser. It got really weird when at some point Jeb said that his brother George kept the country safe. Trump would have none of it. "The World Trade

Center came down during your brother's reign, remember that" he said. "That's not keeping us safe" he added.

At another point in the debate, Trump attacked Jeb on the Iraq war. "Obviously, the war in Iraq was a big fat mistake, all right?" he said. "It took Jeb Bush, if you remember when he announced for president, it took him five days – it was a mistake, it wasn't a mistake, it took him five days before his people told him what to say, and he ultimately said it was a mistake. Obviously it was a mistake. George Bush made a mistake. We can make mistakes. But that one was a beauty." "They lied" he thundered. "They said there were weapons of mass destruction…and they knew there were none". He added the war cost $5 Trillion which could have been used to rebuild America's failing infrastructure.

I couldn't believe what I was watching and hearing. Trump actually said that the Bush administration lied about the Iraq war. The words were coming out of the mouth of a leading contender for the GOP nomination. This was pure heresy. That was how far Trump was willing to go to hurt Jeb Bush.

Trump had some choice words for Senator Marco Rubio from Florida. "Light Weight Marco", "Little Marco", "Mr. Meltdown", "He is a chocker, and once a chocker, always a chocker" were just a few. Throughout the primary, I haven't heard once Trump referring to Marco as "Senator Rubio", "Marco", or "Rubio". It was always "Little Marco" or something worse. Compared to Trump, Senator Rubio was smaller in physique and that is what was so disgusting about Trump mocking Rubio by calling him 'Little Marco".

Carly Fiorina was the only female candidate seeking the Republican Party nomination and Trump couldn't resist attacking her personally. He thrashed her business record which was fine, but that wasn't enough for Trump. He had to go after how she sounds when she speaks. "I think that she's got a good line of pitter-patter. But when you listen for more than five minutes, you develop a tremendous headache" said Trump when he was on "Fox & Friends". He said something very similar during a Sunday interview on ABC's "This Week." That wasn't still enough for Trump. He had to go after Fiorina's looks. On an occasion when he saw Carly being interviewed on TV, Trump's reaction was: "*Look* at that face!" he says "Would anyone *vote* for that? Can you imagine that, the face of our next *president*?!" and he continued "I mean, she's a woman, and I'm not s'posedta say bad things, but really, folks, come on. Are we *serious*?" The man has no bounds and often with a smug face he says "I cherish women."

Let me tell you how Trump dragged the wife and father of Senator Ted Cruz of Texas to the mix of those he personally attacked.

During the first few months of the primary campaign Trump and Cruz did not go after each other. It was as if they had a mutual understanding of some sort. It changed when most of the other candidates suspended their campaigns and Cruz became a threat to Trump.

When the primary was in full swing in Utah, someone or group had posted on Twitter a semi-nude photo of Mrs. Trump taken many years ago when she was pursuing a modeling career. Cruz and his campaign denied any knowledge but Trump apparently was not satisfied. His reaction was to post a photo of Mrs. Cruz on Twitter after having distorted the photo to make her look hideous. To add insult to injury he posted a beautiful photo of Mrs. Trump side by side with Mrs. Cruz's photo. Go figure.

Trump then went after Cruz's father Rafael Cruz using an unsubstantiated tabloid story.

The National Enquirer, a pro-Trump tabloid, carried a story in April, 2016 that it had conclusive evidence of Rafael Cruz being the man photographed next to Oswald in 1963, months before the assassination of President John F. Kennedy.[5]

The photo the tabloid used was from the Warren Commission, in which Oswald is shown passing out pamphlets in New Orleans with men who were not identified by the commission:

No other source corroborated the Enquirer's claim, but it used a testimonial from the CEO of a digitizing photo service, Mitch Gladstone, who has said the man in the photo has "more similarity than dissimilarity" to Cruz and that "...it looks to be the same person and I can say as much with a high degree of confidence."

That tabloid story was sufficient material for Trump to repeat the story. This is how Trump put it:

"His father was with Lee Harvey Oswald prior to Oswald's being — you know, shot. I mean, the whole thing is ridiculous," Trump said.

"What is this, right prior to his being shot, and nobody even brings it up. They don't even talk about that. That was reported, and nobody talks about it."

Trump stopped well short of accusing Cruz's dad of plotting to kill JFK. But he still sought to place the elder Cruz alongside President Kennedy's accused killer.

"I mean, what was he doing — what was he doing with Lee Harvey Oswald shortly before the death? Before the shooting?" Trump said. "It's horrible."

Cruz's campaign responded immediately. "Trump is detached from reality, and his false, cheap, meaningless comments every day indicate his desperation to get attention and willingness to say anything to do so," said campaign spokesperson Catherine Frazier. "We are campaigning on jobs freedom and security while Trump campaigns on false tabloid garbage. And the media is willfully enabling him to cheapen the value of our democratic process."

In a similar way Trump launched vicious personal attacks on his contenders whenever he felt that anyone of them was a threat to him getting the nomination. Actually it was worse than that. Sometimes he went after candidates who didn't pose any threat to him. It was like he was deriving some perverse satisfaction by mocking and ridiculing candidates who were polling in single digits in the national polls. These candidates didn't take it lying down. They too went after Trump mercilessly. Going after Trump though was a fruitless exercise. As long as Trump didn't praise Obama, his base support was rock solid. He had his guaranteed thirty to thirty-five percent of the GOP primary vote. The rest was hopelessly divided.

In primary contests, it's not unusual for bitter rivalry and sometimes vicious attacks being hurled around. But no candidate has ever made mocking, ridiculing and personally insulting other contenders the hallmark of his or her campaign. What is worse, none of it was based on fact. This speaks volumes to the character and modus operandi of the man. I wouldn't want him in the White House. Do You?

Trump and the Media

Over the years Republicans have developed a habit of attacking what they call "the main stream media." There is no better applause line at a Republican rally than an attack on the media. A Republican candidate down in the dumps will get an immediate lift by attacking the media.

Republicans choose not to consider *Rightwing Talk Radio, Fox News channel* and *Wall Street Journal* as part of the media. *Rightwing Talk Radio* and *Fox News Channel* are more or less Republican Party propaganda machines. To their credit they don't even pretend to be neutral. Fox News's "we report you decide" has become a standard joke. Talk Radio viciously attack President Obama and Democrats twenty-four-seven. The way *Fox News* reports,

President Obama and Democrats have never done anything right ever, not even once. It's kind of silly to even consider them as a News Channel. That doesn't take away from the fact that they have the best ratings in the business, sometimes, better than all other prime-time channels combined. That also makes it dangerous. They feed a large part of the audience with their venom on a regular basis. Some of these folks are prone to brain-wash. *Fox News* and *Rightwing Talk Radio* are responsible in large part for the polarization in American society during the last eight years: race against race, religion against religion, and rich against the poor.

Republicans have never been satisfied only having Fox News and rightwing radio in their corner. They habitually demonize the rest of the media as being biased. MSNBC used to be supportive of liberal issues such as minority rights and opposition to wars, but not anymore. In realty, the so called "main stream media' simply report news as it happens. When the news itself favors one side or the other, it makes no sense to blame the reporting media. Republican practice however has been more cunning. Their philosophy is that repetition creates 'make believe.' So, they blame the media all the time. The hope is that everything they report will be considered unworthy. Republicans have been practicing this for a long time. Donald Trump, however, had other ideas and treated media differently.

Trump, always clamoring for good publicity, manipulates the media to his advantage. Just as he pursued the "birther movement" to build for himself a voter-base, Trump seemed to have developed a plan to deal with the media for his presidential campaign. He provided all media with unparalleled access. This is very unusual for a presidential candidate. He even often made unsolicited telephone calls to live TV programs and talk-radio and engaged in conversations. Media loved him for the access he provided and he in turn got his message out. His messages mostly were vicious personal attacks on his fellow candidates or on minorities. He never missed a chance to say what a great rich guy he is, and how he only can make America great again. The media covered his meetings and rallies from start to finish. Anything and everything he wanted covered, the media obliged dutifully. This marriage however was too good to last.

When other GOP candidates started attacking Trump, media relished covering them too. Protesters started appearing at Trump rallies and were getting kicked out. Violence started to break outside Trump rallies. Crude, disgusting and vulgar insults between Trump and other contenders were common place. It was getting ugly and Trump was at the bottom of it all. Media covered these twenty-four-seven and Trump was getting loads of bad publicity. Thin skinned he is, Trump couldn't handle it. His response was to attack the media just as viciously as he attacked fellow candidates and minorities.

Trump went after reporters mercilessly.

It started at the first GOP presidential debate when Megyn Kelly of Fox News pressed Trump about sexist comments he had made in the past, such as calling some women "fat pigs, dogs, slobs, and disgusting animals." He went after her saying her questions were "ridiculous" and "off-base." Trump didn't end it there. It took a totally different turn when on the next day at a TV interview Trump described Kelly at the debate as "You could see there was blood coming out of her eyes", "Blood coming out of her wherever." He subsequently tweeted that he was referring to Kelly's nose, but the remark was widely interpreted as a reference to menstruation.

Another hideous episode was when Trump went after a reporter's physical disability. He had a beef with the reporter when the reporter said he found no evidence of widespread 9/11 celebrations by Muslims in New Jersey as alleged by Trump. At a subsequent rally Trump ridiculed the physical disability of the reporter by jerking his arms and holding one hand at an angle. It was disgusting.

There was no limit to Trump's name calling of reporters. Following are just a few:

"Third-rate reporters, dumbest people in politics, liberal clowns, disasters, dumb bloggers, Dishonest, absolutely terrible, not good people, sleazy, among the worst human beings I have ever met. The press should be ashamed."

It was ugly, but took a turn to the worse when Trump said he wants to "open up" libel laws to punish critics in the news media. This is how he put it at a Fort Worth, Texas rally: "One of the things I'm going to do if I win...[is] I'm going to open up our libel laws so when they write purposely negative and horrible and false articles, we can sue them and win lots of money."

This is scary stuff coming from a guy who wants to be president. Do you want him as your president? I sure don't.

Trump on Policy

Trump isn't a policy guy. Unlike most presidential candidates, he doesn't dwell in national security, economy, foreign policy, education and the like. He prefers to pick issues that his supporters care about. Obama's birth place was such an issue and he built for himself a voter-base with that.

Trump has made his opposition to immigration, terrorism, trade agreements, and America's defense of its allies the cornerstones of his campaign.

Trump only cares for issues which gets him really loud applause at his rallies. The way he sees it:

Immigration is the top issue

National security is terrorism

Economy is trade agreements and tax cuts

Foreign Policy is a bunch of words blaming previous presidents.

He opposes all of them.

Education doesn't get him applause – He doesn't bother with it – Wise!

Immigration

Trump went after immigrants from the get go. He announced his candidacy on June 15, 2015. Following are some excerpts from his speech: [4]

"When do we beat Mexico at the border? They're laughing at us, at our stupidity. And now they are beating us economically. They are not our friend, believe me. But they're killing us economically."

"The U.S. has become a dumping ground for everybody else's problems."

"Thank you. It's true, and these are the best and the finest. When Mexico sends its people, they're not sending their best. They're not sending you. They're not sending you. They're sending people that have lots of problems, and they're bringing those problems with us. They're bringing drugs. They're bringing crime. They're rapists. And some, I assume, are good people".

"But I speak to border guards and they tell us what we're getting. And it only makes common sense. It only makes common sense. They're sending us not the right people".

"It's coming from more than Mexico. It's coming from all over South and Latin America, and it's coming probably— probably— from the Middle East. But we don't know. Because we have no protection and we have no competence, we don't know what's

happening. And it's got to stop and it's got to stop fast".

"I will immediately terminate President Obama's illegal executive order on immigration, immediately".

"I would build a great wall, and nobody builds walls better than me, believe me, and I'll build them very in expensively, I will build a great, great wall on our southern border. And I will have Mexico pay for that wall."

As you could see Trump has deliberately and provocatively insulted an entire ethnic group and has attempted to explicitly scapegoat them.

How true are Trump's claims?

Following are excerpts of a fact check published in The Washington Post on July 8, 2015 by Michelle Ye Hee Lee under the heading "Donald Trump's false comments connecting Mexican Immigrants and crime".[6] The facts disclosed in this article shows that Trump's claim that Mexicans who come to the USA are criminals is baseless.

- Start of Excerpt -

What do the data tell us about the criminal threat of immigrants?

Facts
Data on immigrants and crime are incomplete, but a range of studies show there is no evidence immigrants commit more crimes than native-born Americans. In fact, first- generation immigrants are predisposed to lower crime rates than native-born

Americans. (The Center for Immigration Studies, which advocates for restrictive immigration laws, has a detailed report showing the shortfalls of immigrant crime data)

Immigration and crime levels have had inverse trajectories since 1990s: immigration has increased, while crime has decreased. Some experts say the influx of immigrants contributed to the decrease in crime rates, by increasing the denominator while not adding significantly to the numerator.

-End of Excerpt –

In an interview with NBC's Katy Tur on July 8th, 2015, Trump doubled down that the Mexican government forces many bad people to USA. An article in PolitiFacts by **Louis Jacobson on Thursday, July 9th, 2015 totally debunks Trump's assertion with facts.**[7]

Following are some excerpts from PolitiFacts article:

- Start of Excerpts –

In a July 8 interview with NBC, Republican presidential candidate Donald Trump didn't ease up his rhetoric about Mexican immigration -- at all.

"The Mexican government forces many bad people into our country because they're smart," he told interviewer Katy Tur. "They're smarter than our leaders, and their negotiators are far better than what we have, to a degree that you wouldn't believe. They're forcing people into our country. … And they are drug dealers and they are criminals of all kinds. We are taking Mexico's problems."

Trump left no doubt that he believes the Mexican government is taking an active role in pushing migrants into the United States: He used the word "forcing" four times to describe what the government was doing.

But is it really the government forcing Mexicans across the border, rather than individual decisions to leave, either to seek employment or to join family members in the United States?

A range of immigration experts told PolitiFact that there is no evidence to support Trump's claim. (The Mexican Embassy did not respond to our inquiries, nor did a Trump representative.)

For evidence, let's start with the Mexican Migration Project, a bi-national research effort founded in 1982 to study Mexican migration to the United States. Anthropologists, sociologists and other experts with the project gather data, including field interviews with migrants that illuminate migration patterns.

The co-director of the project is Douglas Massey, a professor of sociology and public policy at Princeton University. Based on more than three decades of field research, Massey finds Trump's assertion to be flat wrong.

He pointed to findings from a paper he published in 2014 in the journal International Migration Review. In the paper, he and his co-authors concluded that undocumented migration from Mexico "was driven largely by U.S. labor demand and by the existence of well-developed migrant networks that provided migrants with access to U.S. labor markets despite a rising enforcement effort. The taking of additional trips is likewise tied to U.S. labor demand and access to migrant networks, as well as the number of U.S. trips a migrant has accumulated over his or her career."

What about Mexican government efforts to push migrants into the United States? Nonexistent, Massey told PolitiFact.

"Mexico has never had a policy of pushing migrants toward the United States, much less 'forcing many bad people into our country,' " Massey said. "Mexican migration is tied to social and economic circumstances on both sides of the border."

.Other experts sided with Massey.

"Immigrants come to work or to join family," said Jeffrey Passel, a senior demographer with the Pew Research Center's Hispanic Trends Project. "And no, the Mexican government doesn't force anyone to leave."

"No, the Mexican government doesn't force anyone to move here illegally, though it certainly doesn't object," added Mark Krikorian, executive director of the Center for Immigration Studies, a group that favors low levels of immigration.

– End of Excerpts –

Trump's Immigration policy

Trump started his campaign calling Mexicans drug

smugglers, criminals and rapists. He promised to build a wall on the southern border and said that he would get Mexico to pay for it. He didn't take long thereafter to announce his plan to round up and deport all eleven million undocumented immigrants – he called them illegal immigrants - living in the United States. His plan also called for the end of automatic citizenship for children born to foreigners on U.S. soil. He outlined these positions in a Sunday television appearance on August 16, 2015 and also in his first campaign policy paper.[8] As of July 2016 Trump hasn't retracted any of the above immigration proposals.

Trump's immigration policy can be easily summarized: Build a wall on the southern border, deport all undocumented immigrants, and shutdown new immigration. That's it.

Trump will build a beautiful wall

"I would build a great wall, and nobody builds walls better than me, believe me, and I'll build them very inexpensively. I will build a great, great wall on our southern border. And I will have Mexico pay for that wall. Mark my words," Trump said in his presidential announcement speech and his supporters went wild.[4]

What's this all about? The US and Mexico share a common border of about 2,000-miles. It's a massive stretch of land and underlines four states from California to Texas. Building a fence along this border to keep out immigrants is not a novel idea. Some are of the view that using more manpower and technology, instead of fencing, would be far more effective to secure the border.

As of February 2012, the Department of Homeland Security had completed 651 miles of fencing out of nearly 652 miles mandated by Congress, including 299 miles of vehicle barriers and 352 miles of pedestrian fence. This is fencing and not the kind of wall that Trump is proposing. He has made himself clear on that, saying, "A wall is better than fencing, and it's much more powerful. It's more secure. It's taller."

How practical it is to build the wall that Trump has promised his supporters?

I have read several opinions as to the practicality of building a wall as envisaged by Trump and haven't come across even one that would say that it would be a practical proposition. Some say that such a wall could never be built. Others are of the opinion that while it may be possible to build the type of wall that Trump refers to, it would be a nonsensical thing even to try.

Following are excerpts from an article by Kriston Capps published in *The Atlantic* CITILAB *in* March 2016 that discusses the possibility of building such a wall. [9]

- Start of Excerpts -

'Details are beside the point, of course. That's because Trump can't build a wall across the entire border. It's a moon-shot without a rocket. The proposal crumbles at even the slightest scrutiny. No one who can build it would, and no one who would build it can.'

'"With the highly contested nature of this project, and the fact that many, many people object to it really strongly—do you want to be on the wrong side of that in a way that's going to stick with you for years?" asks Raphael Sperry, president of Architects/Designers/Planners for Social Responsibility.'

'Sperry says that his organization will condemn the border wall, should Trump be elected president. His organization may not stand alone: Other professional design associations are bound by ethics that Trump's proposal appears to plainly violate. As with other controversial border projects, firms that built this wall could be subject to boycotts, blacklists, and lawsuits.'

'Critics tend to dismiss Trump's chief policy proposal as bonkers. Engineers have never shied away from projects that seem impossible, but walling off Mexico is something worse: It's impractical. Reputational risk, ethical conundrums, and environmental liability each pose significant obstacles to building the project. This wall is a wall unto itself.'

'For most large-scale civil construction projects, and anything involving U.S. waterways, the Corps (The U.S. Army Corps of Engineers) takes the first look. A 2,000-mile border wall, one that crosses the Colorado River and runs alongside (or through?) the Rio Grande, would fall under its regulatory purview. Whether the Corps would take on the building project is harder to say.'

'The Corps would not physically build the wall themselves. For most projects, the Corps engages a "prime" contractor, who then hires on other *subcontractors. A wall running thousands of miles through hills, deserts, and rivers would take a major campaign, possibly involving multiple primes. Not to just to build the wall, but to support the builders: to build the roads that would enable the builders to reach the border. No small feat.'*

'There are just a handful of architectural and engineering firms with the organizational capacity to build Trump's wall. Not the technical know-how— any engineer can design a wall—but rather the experience in management. Marshaling the array of contractors and subcontractors it would take to build a wall across so many different jurisdictions and climate regions would require a fairly elite engineering firm.'

'None of more than a dozen global architecture and engineering firms I contacted were willing to speak on the record about Trump's wall. Neither did faculty at the schools of civil engineering for Texas A&M University and the Georgia Institute of Technology. But several sources pointed to codes of ethics that seek to prevent architects, engineers, and planning professionals from doing harm.'

'The American Institute of Certified Planners, for example, includes in its code of ethics a subsection that reads as strongly at odds with the goal of blocking immigrants from reaching the U.S. through Mexico:

We shall seek social justice by working to expand choice and opportunity for all persons, recognizing a special responsibility to plan for the needs of the disadvantaged and to promote racial and economic integration. We shall urge the alteration of policies, institutions, and decisions that oppose such needs.'

'Building Trump's wall across the Mexican border might require one-tenth of the cement the U.S. produces in an entire year. Maybe more. Maybe all of it.'

'Since the height of the Great Wall of Making America Great Again keeps rising, it's hard to give anything better than a stab in the dark at what it would cost to build, for whoever ends up stuck with the tab. One Daily Kos contributor outlined a plausible-sounding guesstimate regarding the sheer amount of cement it would take to wall off 2,000 miles of mostly natural border.'

'Bill Palmer Jr., the editor of Concrete Construction, offers that a concrete wall running 80 feet high (including 30 feet below grade), 1 foot thick, and 2,000 miles long would require 31 million cubic yards of cement. "If we made it higher-strength concrete, go to 700 pounds per yard, that's 21.7 billion pounds of Portland cement, or about 10 percent of U.S. annual consumption," he writes in an email. Cement is just one ingredient in concrete, and concrete is just one component of a wall-building project.'

'"On a project like this, they would be making their own concrete, so the price would go down," Palmer writes, "but getting materials, equipment, and people to the job site and building this as a government project ([at] prevailing wages) would be very expensive."'
- End of excerpts -

Funding for Trump's beautiful wall

Donald Trump has claimed that he would make Mexico pay for the wall he has proposed building on the southern US border to curb illegal immigration,

In a televised interview in March 2016, Mexico's Finance Minister Luis Videgaray gave the first direct government response to Trump's proposal to build a wall. "Under no circumstances will Mexico pay for the wall that Mr. Trump is proposing," Videgaray said. He said the idea was "based on ignorance and has no foundation in the reality of North American integration." [17]

Mexico's ex-president Vicente Fox's response was more colorful. "I am not going to pay for this f**** wall," Fox said during an interview with journalist Jorge Ramos for Univisión.[18]

In a separate interview with Anderson Cooper on CNN Mr. Fox compared Trump to Hitler. "He is going to take the US back to the old days of conflict, war and everything. I mean, he reminds me of Hitler. That's the way he started speaking," Fox told Cooper in a phone interview. [19]

Felipe Calderon, a conservative who was president of Mexico from 2006 to 2012, went even further than Mr. Fox when he told reporters in February 2016 that Trump's political rhetoric was "racist" and evocative of the Nazi dictator. "This logic of praising the white supremacy is not just anti-immigration," Calderon said. "He is acting and speaking out against immigrants that have a different skin color than he does, it is frankly racist and exploiting feelings like Hitler did in his time," Calderon said. [20]

Trump is threatening the relationship between U.S. and our southern neighbor. It was evident when Mexican President Enrique Peña Nieto publicly condemned Donald Trump's outlandish remarks made about his country. Peña Nieto stated that Trump's statements "are damaging to the relations which Mexico has attempted to establish with the U.S., in the creation of treaties, dialogues and an improvement (in communication), in an attempt to provide solutions for common problems through agreements and shared aims." Interviewed by daily Excelsior, the president said "That's how Mussolini and that's how Hitler rose to power: they made the most of the context, perhaps, in the form of a problem which humanity was experiencing at that point, afterwards this was through an economic crisis." [21]

Trump promises to deport eleven million undocumented immigrants

There are approximately 11.3 million undocumented immigrants in the United States and Donald Trump has promised his supporters that he will deport every single one of them. What's more, he also claims he'll do it all within 18 months to two years. To deport 11 million undocumented immigrants within two years would require the deportation of 5,500,000 people annually.

When pressed how he would accomplish this, he responded that he would follow the example of the military-style roundups authorized by President

Dwight D. Eisenhower in 1954. It was an initiative, known as Operation Wetback, which expelled hundreds of thousands of Mexicans from the U.S. Trump contends that the start of deportations would prompt many to leave on their own, and that it would take about two years to get the job done.

This is pure lunacy. I don't believe neither Trump nor his so called advisors have given five minutes thought to details of all this, because if they did, they would soon realize how stupid the whole thing is.

Michael Chertoff, Secretary of Homeland Security under President George W. Bush had this to say about Trump's proposal: "I can't even begin to picture how we would deport 11 million people in a few years where we don't have a police state, where the police can't break down your door at will and take you away without a warrant." Mr. Chertoff has led immigration enforcement not too long ago.

When the impracticality of his proposal was pointed out, Trump has said that he would triple ICE's (Immigration and Custom Enforcement) deportation officers, to 15,000 from about the current 5000. Trump was ignorant that even such an increase is hopelessly insufficient for what he proposed.

Deportations almost always have to be approved by judges and mass deportations will create huge backlogs.

Arrested immigrants will have to be detained pending deportation which would lead to tens of thousands of people in detention camps.

Millions of immigrants from contiguous countries will have to be bussed and those from noncontiguous nations would have to be flown home.

Arresting these immigrants would be the hardest of all. It has to start with enforcement agents fanning out all over the country looking for undocumented immigrants.

Large scale raids with agents arresting hundreds of workers in their work places would be commonplace.

To find these immigrants, enforcement agents often will have to interrogate U.S. citizens.

Most undocumented immigrants are part of families where some members are U.S. citizens. Those Americans would have to decide whether to stay in their country, separated from their loved ones facing deportation, or leave the U.S.

Where would all this lead us as Americans? Would Americans be coerced in to become immigration informants? Are we to rat on our neighbors? How will women, children and elderly be treated if they have no papers? Is this un-American? We need answers to a whole lot of ugly questions.

Trump proposes to shutdown new immigration

Trump's campaign policy paper on immigration is a document prepared for the explicit purpose of shutting down any and all avenues for immigrants to enter, find work and prosper in the United States. Following are a few excerpts:

'When politicians talk about "immigration reform" they mean: amnesty, cheap labor and open borders.

The Schumer-Rubio immigration bill was nothing more than a giveaway to the corporate patrons who run both parties.

Real immigration reform puts the needs of working people first – not wealthy globetrotting donors.

We are the only country in the world whose immigration system puts the needs of other nations ahead of our own.'

None of this is true, not by a long shot.

The immigration bill Trump is referring to is the **Border Security, Economic Opportunity, and Immigration Modernization Act of 2013** which was passed by the Senate; but was not acted upon by the House of Representatives.

It provided a path for citizenship to undocumented immigrants already in the United States contingent on certain border security and visa tracking improvements and only after legal immigrants waiting for a current priority date receive their permanent residence status. It also provided a different citizenship path for agricultural workers through an agricultural worker program.

It also provided reforms to reduce current visa backlogs and fast track permanent residence for U.S. university immigrant graduates with advanced degrees in science, technology, engineering or math also known as the **STEM fields**.

It also provided for an improved employment verification system for all employers to confirm employee work authorization and improved work visa options for low-skilled workers including an agricultural worker program.

The provisions of this bill had nothing to do with a give away to corporate patrons, and wealthy globetrotting donors or putting the needs of other nations ahead of our own. On the contrary, the provisions of this bill were crafted specifically to meet the needs of working people and our nation. This is the exact opposite of what Trump is claiming.

Let's look at another one of Trump's gems in his policy paper.

'America will only be great as long as America remains a nation of laws that lives according to the Constitution. No one is above the law.

The following steps will return to the American people the safety of their laws, which politicians have stolen from them'

Trump is referring to the eleven million undocumented immigrants. The steps, according to him, that will 'return to the American people the safety of their laws' are the steps that he will take to deport all eleven million undocumented immigrants. That's what he has been saying loud and clear in his interviews and rallies to vast applause of his supporters.

In another proposal in his policy paper, Trump says he wants to "end birthright citizenship," saying it "remains the biggest magnet for illegal immigration". That's not what the research shows.

Marc Rosenblum, deputy director of the U.S. Immigration Policy Program at the Migration Policy Institute, an independent think tank, has told Fact Check.org, a nonpartisan non-profit "consumer advocate" for voters, that research has consistently found economic factors are the big determinants of illegal immigration. "If you read a few hundred academic articles, I don't think you will find one that identifies the desire to have children in the U.S. ... as a significant factor in people's thinking," he said.[10]

What is really behind Trump's Immigration Policy

Immigrants both with documents and undocumented are, like the rest of us, breathing human beings. They are not cattle or some kind of "thing." They leave their country of birth and migrate to another country looking for a better life. Some move through sheer desperation for basic needs such as having a roof above and something to eat. Almost one hundred percent of the time they migrate looking for work. Mr. Trump knows perfectly well that not one immigrant from any part of the world moves to the United States planning to commit crimes. The only exception may be a hired professional assassin, and we know that Trump is not referring to them when he refers to immigrants committing crimes in the U.S.

Immigrants do whatever work they can find, mostly work American citizens do not want to do. You don't need statistics to prove this, just take a close look when you next visit a store or workplace in any type of industry. You will see it for yourself.

Those without documents, "illegals" as Mr. Trump would like to call them, work for whatever pay they can get. They can't complain because they have no "papers" and live in constant fear of being found out and deported. Often, employers take advantage of this and pay them poor wages. Does this contribute to low wages generally? Absolutely, but who is to be blamed? The guy who need to put food on the table for his family or the unscrupulous citizen employer?

Then, there is the sound-bite that undocumented immigrants are a burden to the state and federal governments because they get various kinds of free benefits.

An undocumented immigrant who is an adult (over 18 years of age) be it male or female cannot get a cent worth of freebies from the federal government. Ask an American citizen who has got any kind of free benefits from the federal government the hoops he or she had to jump through. One needs papers to get benefits from the federal government. It's as simple as that. On the contrary, if they are working they may be paying federal taxes and contributions to the social security fund, the benefits of which they will never receive.

The same is true for adults when it comes to state and city benefits except when it comes to medical emergencies. Most undocumented immigrants do not have medical insurance and in emergencies they end up in the emergency ward of the nearest hospital. They don't get kicked out to die, and instead get treatment and the cost more often than not is not met by them and becomes a burden on the city or state.

The children in most states, even of undocumented immigrants get a free education and medical and other benefits. But their parents that work do contribute to the city and state often with city and state taxes and always with sales taxes.

One may wonder how the undocumented immigrants who cannot find work survive. Most don't and return to their countries. Some get help from family members that do work. Community organizations, Churches and charities help. A lot of rich White- Americans also help them ever so quietly.

There is another tragic aspect to the lives of undocumented immigrants. As it's unfortunately common among all humans, undocumented immigrants do get physically and/or mentally abused by their own or documented immigrants or citizens. Sadly, they are reluctant to seek help from authorities through fear of being detected and deported.

Undocumented immigrants are the most vulnerable living among us. Mr. Trump, the strong man, has decided to pick on them. He wants to round up and deport all eleven million of them. He wants to build a beautiful wall so tall that no one can get in. He also wants to stop all other forms of immigration. Why?

I have an answer. I am sure Mr. Trump didn't give two hoots to where President Obama was born, but he pushed the birther issue right to the hilt to build his voter base. Likewise, I don't believe Trump gives two hoots about immigrants one way or the other, but he is pushing the immigration issue because that's where the Republican votes are. What a guy?

National Security

The only national security issue that Trump has seriously addressed in his campaign is terrorism. Terrorism suits his campaign style of fear mongering, anger and desperation. That is also what interests his voters and he puts the fear of god in them with terrorism. I think he kind of enjoys it.
However, we are discussing a presidential election and I have taken the trouble to include a few other aspects of national security which may be useful to voters.

The President of the United States is also the Commander in Chief of its armed forces, the most powerful military in the world. His or her primary duty is to defend the nation against enemies foreign and within. The task is as huge as it's awesome.

Mercifully, the nation is at peace, meaning we are not at war with any country. The world however remains a dangerous place and President Obama has had the wisdom and restraint to avoid direct intervention in troubled nations, and instead help stabilize them by helping their elected governments. To that extent we are engaged in counter terrorism operations in several countries.

Al-Queda and ISIS still remain strong terrorist organizations. They have hijacked a major religion, Islam, claiming to represent an extreme, nonsensical and murderous ideology. They do not respect any life, not even their own as is evidenced by suicide-bombers. These are opportunistic killers who will infiltrate any and all religious sects on the pretext of perpetuating a murderous ideology, whereas their real motive is to grab and remain in power. Their lack of any respect for human life which is their greatest weapon as of now, will ultimately lead to their ruin. It's the responsibility of all nations to destroy them as fast as possible. However, in the process of doing so, every precaution has to be taken not to cause further death and destruction to innocents. This is not easy as these groups live among innocents they brutally terrorize.

Iraq, Afghanistan, and Syria and recently to some extent Libya are often reported in the news media as nations associated with terrorism. This is so misleading. These terrorist groups are also operating in so many other Muslim nations. Turkey, Yemen, Saudi Arabia, Egypt, Tunisia and Algeria are some of them. Terrorists' strategy is to destabilize these countries while engaging in battle against the west. The United States helps every one of these nations in their battle against terrorism. Their armies fight terrorists often with air support from United States and its allies. Wherever possible, they are given weapons, training and help with strategy.

Threats to U.S. National Security

Relations between the US and Russia have deteriorated since Russia annexed Ukraine's Crimea region in 2014 followed by a pro-Russian insurgency in eastern Ukraine. According to our chairman of the Joint Chiefs of Staff, Marine Gen Joseph Dunford, Russia poses the greatest threat to our national security. That was the view expressed by him to the senators during his confirmation hearing in July 2015.

The so called self-radicalized U.S. based lone-wolf terrorists and extremists will continue to pose the most frequent threat to our homeland.

Following are a few excerpts from the opening statement of James R. Clapper, the director of national intelligence, on February 9, 2016 to the senate select committee on intelligence on IC's worldwide threat assessment: [11]

"As I said last year, unpredictable instability has become the "new normal," and this trend will continue for the foreseeable future. Violent extremists are operationally active in about 40 countries."

"There are now some 60 million people who are considered displaced globally."

"Russia and China continue to have the most sophisticated cyber programs. China continues cyber espionage against the United States. Whether China's commitment of last September moderates its economic espionage, remains to be seen. Iran and North Korea continue to conduct cyber espionage as they enhance their attack capabilities."

"Non-state actors also pose cyber threats. ISIL has used cyber to its great advantage, not only for recruitment and propaganda, but also to hack and release sensitive information about US military personnel."

"Al-Qa'ida's affiliates also have proven resilient. Despite counterterrorism pressure that has largely decimated the "core" leadership in Afghanistan and

Pakistan, al-Qa'ida affiliates are positioned to make gains in 2016."

"Turning to weapons of mass destruction, North Korea continues to conduct test activities with concern to United States."

"China continues to modernize its nuclear missile force and is striving for a secure, second-strike capability. It continues to profess a "no first use" doctrine."

"Chemical weapons continue to pose a threat in Syria and Iraq."

"Turning to space and counter-space, there are about 80 countries now engaged in the space domain. Russia and China understand how our military fights and how heavily we rely on space."

"Moscow's military venture into Syria marks its first use since its foray into Afghanistan of significant expeditionary combat power outside the post-Soviet space. Its interventions demonstrate the improvements in Russian military capabilities and the Kremlin's confidence in using them."

- End of Excerpts -

There you have it. Whether we like it or not, that is the world we live in and it's time to examine what Mr. Trump is offering to keep us safe at home and to keep the world at least as safe as it is now, if not safer.

Trump's Proposals on national security and terrorism

So far in his campaign, Mr. Trump has proposed four strategies to improve national security and combat terrorism.

Ban Muslims from entering U.S.
President Obama and Secretary Clinton need to start calling terrorist activities "Islamic terrorism"
Bomb the shit out of ISIS (forgive the French. That is how he says it)
Bring back 'water-boarding' and target families of terrorists

Trump wants to ban Muslims from entering U.S.

On December 7, 2015, Trump called for barring all Muslims from entering the United States. He appeared on live TV and read the following from a piece of paper he held in his hand:

"Donald J. Trump is calling for a total and complete shutdown of Muslims entering the United States until our country's representatives can figure out what is going on,"

It was also released as a campaign press release.

This was in response to the San Bernardino shooting on December 2, 2015 when a married Muslim couple opened fire at a holiday party at the Inland Regional Center in San Bernardino killing 14 people and injuring 22. Most of them were county employees.

Mr. Trump has previously called for surveillance of mosques and has also said he was open to establishing a database for all Muslims living in the U.S.

In the wake of the Orlando massacre at the "Pulse" night club, where a single gunman, again a Muslim, killed fifty people and injured fifty three others, some critically, Mr. Trump made a speech on June 13, 2016 on national security and terrorism. It was also posted on his website.[12]

I saw and heard Mr. Trump make this statement on live T.V. and have also read the transcript several times to make sure that I haven't missed anything. He has placed all blame for recent terrorist attacks on President Obama and Secretary Clinton. Other than that, he has reiterated two of his previously held positions that Muslims should be banned from entering U.S. and the President and Mrs. Clinton should stop being politically correct and call this "Islamic terrorism'.

Trump is obviously aware that the two men who committed these terrible murderous acts at San Bernardino and Orlando were both American citizens born in the U.S. In fact the terrorist that committed the Orlando massacre was born in Queens, New York where Trump himself was also born to immigrant parents.

Mr. Trump says in his speech "The killer, whose name I will not use, or ever say, was born to Afghan parents who immigrated to the United States." He adds "The bottom line is that the only reason the killer was in America in the first place was because we allowed his family to come here. That is a fact, and it's a fact we need to talk about."

But the killer's father immigrated to U.S. over 30 years ago when Ronald Reagan was president. So, what does Mr. Trump want to talk about? That nobody from Afghanistan should ever have been allowed to immigrate to the U.S. That President Reagan and his administration are somehow responsible because they let in a man whose son, who wasn't even born at the time, committed these murders thirty years later. This is idiotic talk, but Trump is not an idiot, he throws these things out in broken English and let them hang out to get votes and that's all it is. It's a shame that no one really calls him on these.

The murder of even one innocent is more than what most Americans could accept. We live in a society where the majority opposes the death penalty. They don't like to see even a brutal murderer being put to death. So, when a large number of innocents are brutally murdered by someone who has never even seen them before, people cannot accept it. The first emotion is fear. Will this happen to us? The next is confusion. Why? These are followed by anger, hatred and need for revenge. Often the perpetrator has also been killed by security forces or has committed suicide. People start looking for someone to turn their anger on, to extract revenge from. A murderer's family is an easy target. Next is his or her ethnic group, more so when they look different. This is when a nation needs real leaders.

There is nothing more despicable than stoking the fears of an injured nation and mobilizing her people's anger against a minority group simply because a brutal murderer lived among that group. That's exactly what Mr. Trump is doing and he needs to stop that. It isn't a good excuse that he is doing it just to get votes.

The harm that Trump causes goes far beyond that. The authorities need information about the murderer and possible accomplices to prevent further harm. Those who are most likely to have that information are within the ethnic minority where the murderer lived. When you scapegoat them, they get frightened and shut themselves off. It's a natural reaction. Trump knows this very well and doesn't care. This doesn't make him just selfish, but dangerous.

Trump's proposal to ban Muslims from entering the U.S. doesn't make any sense. These atrocities have been committed by men who have been born and living in U.S. for years. If Trump's proposal is to round up all Muslims (American citizens included) and send them to wherever he has in mind, just as he wants to round up and deport eleven million undocumented immigrants, then he should stop pussyfooting and say so.

Trump's call to ban Muslims from entering U.S. also causes serious damage in our efforts to fight terrorism. The only practical way to eradicate the terrorist menace is to fight and destroy them in the countries they have a hold on. They are almost exclusively Muslim countries and their governments are fighting terrorists with help from the U.S. and its allies. You don't need to be a rocket scientist to know that calling to ban Muslims doesn't help that effort. What's more, this has already become a recruiting tool for the terrorists. It boosts their claim that

Americans are the enemy of Muslims. Again Mr. Trump doesn't seem to care.

Trump wants to call terrorists acts 'Islamic terrorism'

Trump says to fight ISIS we need to call terrorism they practice as "Islamic terrorism". He asks if President Obama and Secretary Clinton cannot call terrorism by its true name, "Islamic terrorism", how they could possibly fight terrorists.

This is a Republican sound bite to demonize President Obama. It fits well in to their whisper campaign that Obama is a Muslim. This has been going on for some years and Trump has taken it a step further with his favorite words "there is something going on here, folks". He is questioning the President's desire to defeat ISIS alleging Obama has no real interest in defeating them. The 'dog whistle' is getting a little louder.

Does it make a difference if terrorist actions are called "Islamic terrorism"? Will it make the terrorists leave their weapons and go home?

Let's ask the same question in a different way. Why do President Obama and others in his administration not want to call these terrorist acts "Islamic terrorism"? There are several very good reasons.

First of all, they do not want to elevate terrorists by linking their murderous actions to a major religion in the world. This is what the terrorists are yearning for while pursuing a perverse ideology to grab power. What they practice has nothing to do with Islam but attaching themselves to a major religion helps them in so many ways to justify their murderous pursuits.

Second of all, the President and his administration do not want to offend Muslims (there are over a billion of them in the world) by associating their religion with a bunch of murderous terrorists. It's not the right thing to do.

Third of all, Muslims are our allies in the fight against terrorism and only idiots will offend and insult those that fight alongside you.

The real question is does Mr. Trump comprehend all this? Of course he does. He is no fool. So, why does he do it? For votes my friends, for a few lousy votes he will sacrifice all of us.

Trump wants to bomb the shit out of ISIS (forgive the obscenity)

Following are statements by Mr. Trump explaining his plans to defeat Isis:

During a speech at Decker Auditorium in Fort Dodge, Iowa, in November 2015 as described in an article by Pamela Engel on Nov.13, 2015 in Business Insider. [22]

"ISIS is making a tremendous amount of money because they have certain oil camps, certain areas of oil that they took away," Trump said.

He continued: "They have some in Syria, some in Iraq. I would bomb the shit out of 'em. I would just bomb those suckers. That's right. I'd blow up the pipes. ... I'd blow up every single inch. There would be nothing left. And you know what, you'll get Exxon to come in there and in two months, you ever see these guys, how good they are, the great oil companies? They'll rebuild that sucker, brand new — it'll be beautiful."

At a rally in New Hampshire in February 2016 as described by Amanda Prestigiacomo in an article on February 3, 2016 in The Daily Wire. [23]

"If we are attacked, somebody attacks us, wouldn't you rather have Trump as president if we're attacked?" asked Trump. "We'll beat the shit out of them."

"Speaking of potential," transitioned Trump. "I'm not disavowing that [Putin] called me a genius. Are you crazy?"

Back in December, Putin, who is known for having a poor relationship with President Obama, said that Trump was "a really brilliant and talented person, without any doubt." He also praised Trump's willingness for a "more substantial relationship" between Russia and the United States.

"He says he wants to move on to a new, more substantial relationship, a deeper relationship with Russia, how can we not welcome that?" said Putin. "Of course we welcome that."

"Don't worry, I can't be seduced," the real estate mogul added after being seemingly seduced by a sweet-talking Putin.

Mr. Trump then made the point that we should have good relations with Russia and let them "beat the shit out of ISIS also."

"Knock the hell out of [ISIS], but let [Russia] drop some of their bombs that cost $1 million apiece. Let them use some of their weapons that cost billions of dollars," he added.

Similar statements were made by Mr. Trump in some of his other rallies also during the primary season.

That was when he was battling for the Republican Party nomination. He is now the nominee and has not retracted any one of those statements, if anything he has doubled down. He got wild applause from his crowds for those lines, but what do they really mean?

American forces do bomb and kill ISIS terrorists in Iraq, Syria and wherever else it's possible. They also bomb and destroy in a measured way oil fields and pipelines that finance ISIS. These attacks are made in coordination with local ground forces for maximum effect. Avoiding collateral damage is a huge part of this effort. Good intelligence is believed to be the key. Loss of innocent life causing vast discontent within local communities could effectively nullify the value of the mission. It's a hard balancing act that our forces are engaged in and these raids are continuing causing severe damage to ISIS. As far as regaining ground and diminishing areas of the so called Arab Caliphate, the local forces in Iraq and Syria are winning with air support, intelligence, and strategy from American forces and its allies. That is and has been the American policy since the emergence of ISIS.

So, what exactly is Mr. Trump proposing?

These are matters of life and death. In San Bernardino, California and Orlando, Florida we lost ninety four innocent American lives. Hundreds are brutally murdered in Western European countries who are our allies. Thousands are being massacred in Muslim countries. We are fighting alongside them to defeat ISIS.

So, what does he mean when he says "Bomb the shit out of ISIS"? Does he mean carpet bomb areas occupied by ISIS thereby killing hundreds of thousands of innocent civilians?

"Bomb the shit out of their oil fields" says Mr. Trump. Does he mean totally destroy all Iraq oil fields? In an interview with CNN's Anderson Cooper on July 8, 2015 Cooper asked him about the potential consequences of such an action. Trump just repeated himself "I would bomb the hell out of those oil fields. I wouldn't send many troops, because you won't need them by the time I'm finished."

What are we to do with this? They resemble the utterances of a half-drunk pinhead boasting to a bunch of his fully drunk friends in a cheap bar. Never the less, he remains the nominee of the Republican Party for the president of the United States. His supporters adore him.

Trump wants to bring back 'water-boarding' and target families of terrorists

Throughout his campaign and several times during Republican presidential debates Trump advanced the position that 'water-boarding' should be brought back as a method of interrogating terrorist suspects. His supporters loved it.

Then at a Fox News' Fox and Friends interview on December 3, 2015 he went a step further and asserted that the United States should also target the families of terrorists.[24] This is how he put it in his own words:

"The other thing with the terrorists is you have to take out their families, when you get these terrorists, you have to take out their families. They care about their lives, don't kid yourself. When they say they don't care about their lives, you have to take out their families," Trump said.

To give Trump his due he is pretty clear on his positions on water-boarding and targeting terrorists' families. Equally clear, he wants to bring us down to the same level as terrorists. What's good enough for them is good enough for us. Go figure!

To be fair by Trump, at least on water-boarding, according to some polls a majority of Americans say torturing terrorists is acceptable in some circumstances. Go figure that as well!

Torture is illegal by our laws and is also illegal by international laws. There has been a never ending debate whether 'water-boarding' amounts to torture.

President Obama made the argument mute by declaring water-boarding illegal.

The bottom line is American security forces will not carryout illegal acts even if a president were to order them. So, why is a candidate seeking the presidency spending his time on torture and targeting terrorists' families? For votes my friends anything to get votes.

Economy

When he addresses the U.S. economy Trump concentrates on trade agreements, tax cuts and deregulation.

Trade Agreements

"We have lost our good jobs because of trade agreements", that is Trump's punch line on Hillary Clinton when discussing the economy. He blames Hillary and Obama for all trade agreements. That fits well with his campaign of fear, anger and desperation.

He is pretty good at riling low waged workers. He would have preferred if they couldn't find any work at all, but unfortunately for him, with the unemployment rate below 5 percent most people have jobs. Some actually do two or three jobs to make ends meet. Trump is right in that quite a lot of good paying jobs have vanished.

There is no valid reason to blame Hillary for the jobs that have disappeared. But, then, Trump doesn't need good reason for most things he says and does. His supporters are fine with that. But what is not fine is to feed a false narrative and make bogus promises to folks who are struggling.

Trump made a speech on trade in Monessen, Pennsylvania on June 28, 2016. In his speech he describes seven steps that he says he would pursue to bring back jobs. [25]

"A Trump administration will change our failed trade policies, and I mean quickly.

Thank you. Here are seven steps I would pursue right away to bring back our jobs.

Number one, I am going to withdraw the United States from the Trans-Pacific Partnership, which has not yet been ratified.

I am going to appoint the toughest and smartest, and I know them all, trade negotiators to fight on behalf of American workers.

I am going to direct the secretary of commerce to identify every violation of trade agreements a foreign country is currently using to harm you, the American worker.

I will then direct all appropriate agencies to use every tool under American and international law to end these abuses. And abuse is the right word.

Number four. I'm going to tell our NAFTA partners that I intend to immediately renegotiate the terms of that agreement to get a better deal by a lot. Not just a little, by a lot for our workers.

And if they don't agree to a renegotiation, which they might not because they are so used to having their own way — not with Trump they won't have their own way.

Then, I will submit under Article 2205 of the NAFTA Agreement that America intends to withdraw from the deal.

Number five. I'm going to instruct my treasury secretary to label China a currency manipulator, which should have been done years ago.

Any country that devalues their currency in order to take unfair advantage of the United States, which is many countries, will be met with sharply. And that includes tariffs and taxes.

Number six, I'm going to instruct the U.S. trade representative to bring trade cases against China, both in this country and at the WTO.

China's unfair subsidy behavior is prohibited by the terms of its entrance to the WTO and I intend to enforce those rules and regulations. And basically, I intend to enforce the agreements from all countries, including China.

Seven, if China does not stop its illegal activities, including its theft of American trade secrets, I will use every lawful — this is very easy. This is so easy. I love saying this. I will use every lawful presidential power to remedy trade disputes, including the application of tariffs consistent with Section 201 and 301 of the Trade Act of 1974, and Section 232 of the Trade Expansion Act of 1962."

Let's examine his seven steps.

Number One:

Number one is the **Trans-Pacific Partnership (TPP).** Trump says he is going to withdraw United States from this partnership. That is fine. The only problem is he is clearly misleading folks when he says it will bring back jobs. We haven't lost any jobs because of TPP. It's not even in effect yet. Like he says U.S. hasn't even ratified it.

What he hasn't told the people is what TPP really is.

Twelve states that between them represent 40 percent of the global economy have over a span of years negotiated the Trans-Pacific Partnership. They are home to 800 million people, representing 12 percent of global population.

The twelve countries to the partnership are Australia, Canada, Japan, Malaysia, Mexico, Peru, United States, Vietnam, Chile, Brunei, Singapore and New Zealand

This is obviously a big deal but will come into effect only after the governments of the member nations have ratified it. Whether it will happen is uncertain at this time. In the United States alone there is serious opposition to TPP, more from the Democrats than from the Republicans. President Obama who is a strong supporter of TPP may not be successful in garnishing enough support to get it passed through Congress. I am sure he was banking on solid support from Republicans to get it through, but now with strong opposition from their presidential nominee Mr.

Trump it's up in the air. Mrs. Clinton supported TPP when she was the secretary of state, but now has come out against it. I have no personal knowledge of this, but it's safe to assume that she was cornered in to this position by her opponent Bernie Sanders during the Democratic Party primary. Bernie hated TPP and bitterly criticized it as a job killer.

Numbers Two and Three:

These are gibberish. Trump trying to rattle his listeners with thrash talk with no real meaning. He is pretty good at it. I am sure he got plenty applause for these lines. They are not going to bring any jobs back.

Number Four:

Trump wants to renegotiate NAFTA terms. That's what President Obama said when he was campaigning in 2008. It didn't happen. Trump says he will go a step further. That if the partners refuse to renegotiate, Trump says he will withdraw from the deal.

North Atlantic Free Trade Agreement (NAFTA) was signed by President Clinton in December 1993 and took effect on January 1, 1994. That was 22 years ago.

I am not an economist and am not going to discuss merits or otherwise of NAFTA. Real economists with solid reputations disagree hopelessly on this issue.

However, to say with certainty that withdrawing from NAFTA will bring jobs back to U.S. is a stretch. On the contrary, according to some economists America may lose jobs. There is universal agreement that the American consumer will be affected adversely.

Number Five:

Trump promises to label China a currency manipulator if he is elected. This was also the position of Mitt Romney when he ran for president in 2012.

The Treasury had listed China as a currency manipulator in 1994 under the Clinton administration, which status had been subsequently lifted.

Obama administration contends that the U.S. is more likely to make progress on economic issues with China through negotiation than confrontation.

It's above my pay grade to express an opinion on the advisability of labeling China as a currency manipulator at any given time. All I could say is that it would be wise for any president to heed the advice of his treasury secretary and economists on a matter of this nature. As for Mr. Trump, he has already made the decision well in advance and will be guided by his own thoughts than by the advice of experts.

Numbers Six and Seven

Trump wants to bring trade cases against China. I believe, if elected, he would. He is known to have been fond of litigation. Furthermore he has expressed a personal resentment towards China calling those who govern that nation thieves and robbers. I am sure he will enjoy suing them irrespective of the merits of any case. I have no idea what good that would do or how it would help bring jobs back to America.

Those conclude Trumps seven steps to bring jobs back to U.S.

Tax Cuts

In September 2015 Trump released his tax plan which is loaded for the rich.[14]

Currently, the top income tax rate for regular income is 39.6 percent. Mr. Trump would cut that rate to 25 percent, the lowest level since 1931. He'd cut maximum rates on capital gains and dividends to 20 percent from 23.8 percent. He'd cut the corporate tax rate to 15 percent, and also offer a special tax rate of 15 percent to business owners — less than half what they may pay under today's rules. He'd abolish the estate tax entirely.

By most estimates his proposed tax cuts could mean about $12 trillion less in federal revenue in the first 10 years after they took effect.

We all know what happened with George W. Bush's tax cuts. But we needn't go by that.

Moody's Analytics is arguably the most respected economic analysis company in the world and have done an analysis of Trump's proposed economic policies and reached the following conclusions: [15]

'Conclusions:

Presidential candidates often put forward proposals that are as much political statements as firm policy positions. No one expects that their proposals will get through the legislative process and into law fully intact. But while the policy proposals put forward by candidates are generally well overstated, they are a statement on their philosophy and priorities.

Mr. Trump's economic policy proposals should be considered through this lens. He has suggested that he might be willing to bend his position on taxes and perhaps tariffs. He has even intimated that his policy statements are simply a negotiating stance— he is asking for a lot more up front than he ultimately expects to get.

Having said this, what he is asking for is fiscally unsound. His tax and spending proposals will result in very large deficits and a much higher debt load. A future Congress may be able to rein in this profligacy, but it will not be easy, as there is a gulf between what he says he wants on taxes and spending and what it will take to make the budget arithmetic work.

He is also very suspicious of globalization. His willingness to threaten higher tariffs on U.S. trading partners and his sharp criticism of major trade deals signal a reversal on the long-running expansion of U.S. trade and foreign investment. Requiring millions of undocumented immigrants to leave the country also signals less openness to the rest of the world.

The upshot of Mr. Trump's economic policy positions under almost any scenario is that the U.S. economy will be more isolated and diminished.'

- End of Conclusions -

Deregulation

Irrespective of consequences, Republicans are always for deregulation. Trump is no different and proposes to weaken Wall Street reforms and dismantle most of the Dodd-Frank financial regulations.

It wasn't that long ago that we experienced the craving for short-term efficiency turn into long-term disaster as we approached the Meltdown of 2008. One would think that the absolute havoc it created among so many members of the middle class would have been a lesson to us all. Not so for Republicans. They are back at again praising deregulation.

Foreign Policy

"The Center for the National Interest" based in Washington DC is a think tank established by former president Richard Nixon in 1994. It used to be called the 'Nixon Center' and was renamed in 2011. On their invitation Mr. Trump made his foreign policy speech at their Center on April 27, 2016. [16]

It's a pathetic effort at a foreign policy speech, delivered at a think-tank, perhaps mistaking the venue for one of his rowdy rallies. It's a never ending rant full of right-wing talking points.

He calls all U.S. presidents since Ronald Reagan total disasters.

He is particularly harsh on George W. Bush for the Iraq war which he says began with the dangerous idea that we could democratise countries that have no interest in becoming western democracies.

He blames Barack Obama for the uprisings in Egypt and Libya that threw out their dictators. He is blaming

Obama for not helping the two dictators to brutally crush their citizens who were aspiring for freedom.

Trump calls America a disaster with a weak economy and a weak military. We have a volunteer army ready to lay down their lives for us and he calls them disasters at his rallies. He insulted all our P.O.W.s by insulting Senator McCain. According to him McCain was no good because he got caught to the enemy. Trump says he respects those that doesn't get caught. According to Trump McCain was called a war hero only because he got caught and became a prisoner.

He says President Obama is not a friend of Israel and treats Iran with tender care and love.

He blames invasion of Iraq for emergence of ISIS and in the same breath blames Obama for not going to war with Syria.

And the list goes on endless.

After a long litany of complaints against President Obama, he sets out the following as his goals as president:

"These are my goals, as president.

I will seek a foreign policy that all Americans, whatever their party, can support, and which our friends and allies will respect and welcome.

The world must know that we do not go abroad in search of enemies, that we are always happy when old enemies become friends, and when old friends become allies.

To achieve these goals, Americans must have confidence in their country and its leadership again.

Many Americans must wonder why our politicians seem more interested in defending the borders of foreign countries than their own.

Americans must know that we are putting the American people first again. On trade, on immigration, on foreign policy – the jobs, incomes and security of the American worker will always be my first priority.

No country has ever prospered that failed to put its own interests first. Both our friends and enemies put their countries above ours and we, while being fair to them, must do the same.

We will no longer surrender this country, or its people, to the false song of globalism.

The nation-state remains the true foundation for happiness and harmony. I am skeptical of international unions that tie us up and bring America down, and will never enter America into any agreement that reduces our ability to control our own affairs.

NAFTA, as an example, has been a total disaster for the U.S. and has emptied our states of our manufacturing and our jobs. Never again. Only the reverse will happen. We will keep our jobs and bring in new ones. There will be consequences for companies that leave the U.S. only to exploit it later.

Under a Trump Administration, no American citizen will ever again feel that their needs come second to the citizens of foreign countries.

I will view the world through the clear lens of American interests.

I will be America's greatest defender and most loyal champion. We will not apologize for becoming successful again, but will instead embrace the unique heritage that makes us who we are.

The world is most peaceful, and most prosperous, when America is strongest.

America will continually play the role of peacemaker.

We will always help to save lives and, indeed, humanity itself. But to play that role, we must make America strong again.

We must make America respected again. And we must make America great again.

If we do that, perhaps this century can be the most peaceful and prosperous the world has ever known.

Thank you."

What emerges clearly from his goals is that Trump is against globalism and that he is all for protectionism and nationalism. Indeed, that has been his message throughout his campaign.

Taken in its entirety it's a speech by a man who hasn't taken the trouble to sit with his foreign policy advisors and craft a vision for the nation he is seeking to lead. Instead he has considered it adequate to rant for hours repeating right-wing conservatives' rhetoric. He has said several times in interviews that on any matter, he relies on the ideas that naturally comes in to his head and doesn't need advisors.

What's most offensive is the ease with which he demonizes America and her position in the world. It's heartbreaking that notwithstanding the damage he is already causing, a considerable section of Republicans are still willing to back this man.

The Endgame

It's time to conclude 'Why not Trump?"

Wherever possible, I have presented Trump to you in his own words.

I have followed Trump's campaign very closely, listened to almost all his speeches, followed his rallies and watched him perform in all GOP primary debates except the one he didn't participate because he couldn't handle Megyn Kelly of Fox News.

We have seen Trump starting his campaign as far back as 2011 with a bogus claim that President Obama was not born in the U.S.

He has followed it up with disgusting personal insults on his fellow Republican candidates. He even insinuated that the father of a fellow GOP candidate, Senator Ted Cruz was somehow connected to the assassination of President John F. Kennedy.

He has a history of insulting women. What's worse, it's obvious that he relishes doing that.

In a 2006 feud involving Miss USA, he called Rosie O'Donnell an "animal," an "extremely unattractive person," and a "slob."

Trump had once told a contestant on NBC's Celebrity Apprentice it would be a pretty picture to see her on her knees.

You see the ugly mean streak in him when he went after Arianna Huffington in 2012 with a tweet: Huffington "is unattractive both inside and out. I fully understand why her former husband left her for a man – he made a good decision."

He even went after his only female GOP opponent Carly Fiorina about how bad her face looks.

This is only a small sample of how viciously he has treated celebrity women and it isn't hard to imagine how he would treat an ordinary woman who dared cross his path.

We have observed him enjoying himself while attacking entire minority communities and promising to round up and forcibly deport 11 million undocumented immigrants.

We have seen him insulting our trading partners China, Mexico, South Korea, Japan and Vietnam by calling them cheats, thieves and robbers.

He has tried to damage our relationships with Muslim nations who are our allies in the fight against terrorism.

We have seen him stoking fear in our communities after heinous terrorist attacks.

He has suggested that we are wasting our money and resources with NATO and United Nations.

He has complained that we are wasting our money defending our allies and its o/k for Japan, South Korea and Saudi Arabia to go nuclear.

He wants libel laws to be amended so that he could sue and punish his critics in the news media and make loads of money.

He wants to shutout an entire class of immigrants and visitors to U.S. solely on the basis of their religion.

He has never condemned or discouraged violence at his rallies. Instead, Trump encouraged them with winks and nods.

I now have a very clear understanding of how Mr. Trump operates. Obviously, what is included in this chapter is only a fraction of his campaign, but I believe I have included enough of it, for you to be able to get a clear understanding of who he is really like.

The way I see it, Mr. Trump is running on a platform focused on immigration and protectionism. With a toxic mix of lies, intimidation, vulgarity, hostility to criticism, and disposition to violent intimidation, Mr. Trump is trying appeal to the basic fear in human beings. I don't believe he will succeed but he definitely has managed to poison the 2016 presidential election.

We are the strongest nation in the world. America can survive not one, but many of the likes of Mr. Trump. But why invite catastrophe even for one term?

I have a question:

Are we going to handover this beautiful country to a guy, who by his own words proved to be a racist and a serial liar? One who has questioned the impartiality of an American born judge because his parents were born in Mexico? And one who has pledged to ban all Muslims from entering U.S. – 1.6 billion members of an entire religion?

Chapter 5

Why Hillary?

"Do all the good you can. By all the means you can. In all the ways you can. In all the places you can. At all the times you can. To all the people you can. As long as ever you can." [1]
John Wesley

That is the admonition of John Wesley, the founder of Methodism. There are a little over 7 million Methodists in the United States and Hillary Rodham Clinton is one of them.
Her biographer Carl Bernstein in his book *A Woman in Charge*[22] says Hillary learned of Wesley's admonition when she was a teenager.

I have followed Hillary's public life since her husband Bill ran for president in 1992. John Wesley would be proud of her.

Personal Life
The eldest child and only daughter of Hugh and Dorothy Rodham, Hillary was born in Chicago, Illinois on October 26, 1947.

Her only siblings are the two younger brothers Hugh and Tony.

Hillary and Bill's only child is their daughter Chelsea. They are the grandparents of Chelsea's two kids Charlotte and Aidan.

Hillary graduated from Wellesley College, Wellesley, Massachusetts in 1969 and earned a J.D. from Yale Law School, New Haven, Connecticut in 1973.

Hillary met Bill Clinton at Yale where they were both students and were married in Fayetteville, Arkansas in October 1975.

Public Service

Bill's life as a public servant started in 1976 when he was elected Attorney General of Arkansas. Hillary joined two years later in 1978 when Bill was elected Governor of Arkansas.

Hillary was Arkansas' first lady from 1979 to 1981 and 1983 to 1992 and she left the governor's mansion in 1993 to move in to the White House as the nation's First lady.

As Bill was completing his second term as president in 2000, Hillary was campaigning for the United States senate seat in New York, vacated by Liberal giant Daniel Patrick Moynihan. Hillary won easily defeating Republican Rick Lazio by more than 800,000 votes. She is the first First Lady elected to the United States Senate and the first woman elected statewide in New York.

Hillary's campaign in 2008 for the nomination of the Democratic Party for president of the United States didn't go her way. At the end of a hard fought contest she lost narrowly to the Junior Senator from Illinois Barack Obama. She was a graceful loser. Within days she put her wholehearted support behind Obama. She held nothing back and went all the way lock stock and barrel for Obama.

In November 2008 Obama won in a landslide and invited Hillary to be his Secretary of State. Hillary served as the 67th Secretary of State of the United States from January 2009 to February 2013.

In April 2015, Hillary officially announced her campaign for the Democratic Party presidential nomination in 2016. This time she won easily. It was a battle with the Junior Senator from Vermont, Bernie Sanders. He was an Independent and joined the Democratic Party in 2015 prior to declaring his candidacy. Though an Independent, Bernie always caucused with Democrats. On a few issues Bernie is to the left of Hillary. Otherwise, on policy, there isn't much daylight between the two of them. Even after all the states have voted and Hillary clearly had all the delegates she needed to win the nomination, Bernie held back his endorsement of Hillary until he squeezed as much concessions as possible in the Democratic Party platform to be adopted at the convention. Hillary was very gracious to him both during and after the campaign. Bernie was successful in getting some of his agenda in to the party platform and Hillary was rewarded with a wholehearted endorsement and support from Bernie. Hillary needs those Bernie voters and it looks like it will work out fine.

It has been a long 37 years in public service since Hillary entered the Governor's mansion in 1979 as

Arkansas' First Lady. She has had her share of ups and downs.

Her husband lost his governorship in Arkansas in 1981 only to regain it back in 1983.
In December 1998 President Bill Clinton was impeached by the House of Representatives on two articles of impeachment charging him with lying under oath to a federal grand jury and obstructing justice. It all started with Bill having sexual encounters with a 21- year old intern in the White House. In February 2009, at a senate hearing, the president was acquitted on both articles of impeachment. Even at the height of his impeachment Bill Clinton remained a popular president. But that obviously didn't help the pain and embarrassment endured by Hillary and Chelsea who was a teenager at the time. It also didn't help that there had been previous allegations of sexual indiscretion by Bill going back to the days in Arkansas.
To be fair by Bill, with all his indiscretions, he was an excellent president. He genuinely loved people and people loved him. The saying was 'he could feel their pain'. He could communicate with ordinary Americans like no other politician could. He has a brilliant mind and Americans did very well under his presidency.

When George H.W. Bush was elected after the two terms of Ronald Reagan, Republicans had this feeling that they owned the White House. 'Democrats may hold the Congress, but the White House is ours' it was like their right. Neither Republicans nor Conservatives believed that, with Ross Perot notwithstanding, George H.W. Bush will not be reelected for a second term. Who could blame them? Not long before the election his approval rating was polling in the nineties. That was the first Iraq war effect.

When Bill was elected president, Republicans were shocked. Then, they had Hillary to contend with.

Hillary's stands on children's issues, race relations, healthcare and women's issues made her a rising star in the Democratic Party. It didn't go unnoticed by the Republicans and Conservatives. They unleashed a campaign to bring both Bill and Hillary down. They still have a go at Bill now and then, but the campaign against Hillary is now on steroids.

Hillary is now the Democratic Party nominee for president in 2016. And she is also the most famous woman in the world.

Hillary is where she is today for five good reasons:
She is passionate.
She is a fighter.
She never gives up.
She works like a horse, and
She abides by John Wesley's admonition.

The good that has Hillary done

Many books and articles have been written about Hillary Clinton by folks who admire her. Even more have been published by those who immensely dislike her. With 37 years in public life, that's to be expected. I am sure most of you have already read quite a bit about Hillary elsewhere.

Hillary's father was a diehard Republican and so was Hillary when she was a teenager. At Wellesley

College she was elected president of the Young Republicans Club. However, by 1966 Hillary's political views had started to change. Her opposition to the Vietnam War apparently had a lot to do with it. Hillary had actually met Dr. Martin Luther King and his killing had traumatized her. Her transformation from a Young Republican to a Liberal Democrat had been completed in Yale Law School.

This chapter is not a Biography of Hillary. It's very much limited to examining her actions and experience which, at least in my humble view, eminently qualifies her to be the president of the United States.

An action is worth a thousand words.

In the following pages I'll be referring to some actions Hillary has taken over the years.

Children's issues and women's rights

Children's issues and Women's rights are and have been two of Hillary Clinton's pet issues.

There are 74.2 million children (under age 18) in the United States. Worldwide, the only statistic I could find was for 2004 and that is for children under age 15. There were 1826 million kids in 2004 and they made up a third of the world population. [2] More or less every adult agrees that most kids in the world, and that includes the United States, need a lot more help than they are getting now. Hillary has made it her business to do what she can. I don't believe that even her ardent critics dispute that.

There are slightly more women in the United States than men. World taken as a whole, there are slightly more men than women. There is no getting away from the fact that in real life women do not have the same benefits and opportunities available to men, nor do they have equal legal rights. This is universal. Even in the United States, in 2016, women have lesser rights than men. Hillary, throughout her adult life, has fought for equal rights for girls and women. This has won her immense admiration from many. It sure has also drawn bitter criticism from some Republicans and Conservatives.

Hillary Clinton has been interested in children's issues from her college days. She had volunteered at Yale's Child Study Center, learning about new research on early childhood brain development [3]

Also as a college student she has volunteered at New Haven Hospital, where she took on cases of child abuse and at the city Legal Services, providing free legal service to the poor. [3]

As far back as 1973, the year she graduated from Yale, Hillary wrote an article for the Harvard Educational Review concerning the lack of sufficient legal rights for children. Following is an excerpt from that article: [4]

'Adult Americans enjoy the legal rights set forth in the Constitution, statutes, regulations, and the common law of the federal and state governments. Child citizens, although their needs and interests may be greater than those of adults, have far fewer legal rights (and duties). Indeed, the special needs and interests which distinguish them from adults have served as the basis for not granting them rights and

*duties, and for entrusting enforcement of the few
rights they have to institutional decision-makers. . . .'*

This article earned her fierce criticism from some
Republicans and Conservatives.

Upon graduation from Yale Law School Hillary went to
work as a staff attorney for the Children's Defense
Fund, in Cambridge, Massachusetts. In later years
she has also served as a board member and
chairwoman of the Children's Defense Fund.

Children's Defense Fund is a private, nonprofit
organization supported by individual donations,
foundations, corporate and government grants. Their
mission is to ensure every child a *Healthy Start*, a
Head Start, a *Fair Start*, a *Safe Start* and a *Moral
Start* in life and successful passage to adulthood with
the help of caring families and communities. [5]

After her move to Arkansas, Hillary co-founded the
Arkansas Advocates for Children and Families in
1977. The group's mission is to ensure that all
children and their families have the resources and
opportunities to lead healthy and productive lives and
to realize their full potential. [6]

Also in 1977 President Jimmy Carter appointed Hillary
to the board of Legal Services Corporation. [6]

From 1986 to 1992 Hillary served as the chair of the
Children's Defense Fund. [7]

From 1988 to 1992 Hillary served on the board of
the Arkansas Children's Hospital.[8]

When Bill Clinton was elected Arkansas governor in
1979, he appointed Hillary to be the chairwoman of
Arkansas' Rural Health Advisory Committee — a

group that worked to expand health care access within the state's large rural population.[8]

In 1982, Bill Clinton named Hillary as chair of the Arkansas Educational Standards Committee.[9]

After serving as Arkansas First lady for twelve years, Hillary Clinton moved to the White House in January 1993 as the nation's First Lady.

In his 1992 presidential election Bill Clinton campaigned heavily on healthcare. Soon after his inauguration as president Bill put Hillary in charge of a task force to devise a plan for comprehensive health care. They came up with a plan to provide universal healthcare to all Americans. It was called the Health Security Act. Those who opposed the plan nicknamed it "Hillarycare". Republicans, Conservatives and Libertarians, heavily backed by the pharmaceutical and health insurance industries, opposed the plan vehemently. Democrats tried different versions of it to no avail and the whole effort died by September 1994. This was a huge setback for the Clinton Administration and a personal loss for Hillary Clinton. What is worse, it is generally believed that the failed effort at healthcare was the main reason behind the heavy losses suffered by the Democrats in the 1994 Congressional elections. They in fact lost the majority in the House.

But Hillary didn't give up. She joined forces with U.S. Senator Ted Kennedy from Massachusetts and worked relentlessly to get a health insurance program for children. Success at last, they got it done. It was another hard fought battle. This was a big deal for children. Apparently, it now covers more than eight million low income kids across the nation.

David Nexon was Ted Kennedy's healthcare staff director at the time. Following is an account by Mr. Nixon which refers to Hillary's contribution to the effort.[10]

By David Nexon
Senator Ted Kennedy's former healthcare staff director:

I was there when Hillary Clinton helped lead the bipartisan effort to create the Children's Health Insurance Program.

As Senator Ted Kennedy's health care staff director, I had a front-row seat to the decades-long battle he fought to give every American access to quality, affordable health care. And thanks to his passion and his leadership, we were able to achieve some great things—even in the face of staunch Republican opposition—including health care reform and the creation of the Child Health Insurance Program. But Senator Kennedy didn't wage this fight alone; he had a key ally inside the Clinton administration.

Hillary Clinton was there when it counted. As Senator Kennedy said, "The children's health program wouldn't be in existence today if we didn't have Hillary pushing for it from the other end of Pennsylvania Avenue."

It's well known that as first lady, Hillary worked hard in pursuit of something that progressives had been seeking for generations: universal health care.

But you might not remember that after Republicans and special interests defeated the Clinton administration's effort to pass national health insurance in 1994, Hillary refused to give up—and she turned her attention to other ways to help expand health care for American families.

Senator Kennedy and Senator Orrin Hatch together created the bipartisan plan to provide comprehensive health insurance to millions of children that became known as CHIP. Passing that program—a new entitlement—in a Gingrich-led Republican Congress was an incredible achievement, and it was one that wouldn't have been successful without Mrs. Clinton's commitment and hard work. As Nick Littlefield, Senator Kennedy's top domestic policy adviser, said, Hillary was "a one-woman army inside the White House to get this done."

Under Hillary's leadership, the White House was there at three crucial moments that made all the difference. First, Senator Kennedy and others worked with the then–first lady to have President Clinton call for expanded coverage for children in the 1997 State of the Union and to include a children's coverage policy in his budget proposal.

Second, when the Clinton administration negotiated the 1997 Balanced Budget Act with the Republican Congress, Hillary pushed for it to include billions of dollars in children's health insurance—a program the Republican leadership strongly resisted. They wanted to cut back existing health programs like Medicare and Medicaid, not create new ones.

Finally, Senators Hatch and Kennedy pushed the amount for child health insurance up to $24 billion in the Senate Finance Committee mark-up of the Balanced Budget Act; Hillary directed the *administration to fight for the full $24 billion in the conference with the House, and she was successful. This was no easy task, since the House Republicans were predisposed not to expand the program and only wanted the $16 billion proposal passed in the House. And as part of that critical negotiation, it was the White House, guided by Hillary that made sure that children were guaranteed that the coverage they would receive under the program was both comprehensive and affordable.*

But even with the new program signed into law, the work wasn't done—and Hillary knew it.

It was up to the states to make sure low-income children could enroll and receive high-quality care. Hillary worked alongside Republican governors across the country, including Pennsylvania Gov. Ridge, New Jersey Gov. Whitman, and Utah Gov. Leavitt to promote the Insure Kids Now campaign and make sure the children who needed coverage were able to sign up.

Today, CHIP covers more than 8 million low-income children across the country—all thanks to a program that Hillary helped to enact.

- End of Mr. Nexon's Account –

In her role as First Lady Hillary Clinton had visited 82 countries. In those visits she hadn't missed an opportunity to hammer her pet issues of childcare and women's rights.

Women's rights or the lack thereof was gaining ground in the 1970s and the United Nations had organized four world conferences on women. The first was held in Mexico City in 1975, followed by the second in Copenhagen in 1980. The third conference took place in Nairobi in 1985 and the fourth and the last after ten years was to be held in Beijing in 1995.

Hillary wanted to lead a delegation to the conference in Beijing, but apparently White House was not comfortable that the first lady ought to be travelling to Beijing at a time when the relations between United States and China weren't the best. There is a fine article by Mattie Khan published in the ELLE magazine on Sep 8, 2015 with a detailed account of Hillary's appearance at the Beijing conference and following are some excerpts: [11]

"It was tenuous," admits Melanne Verveer, who then served as Chief of Staff to Hillary Clinton in the White House. "A lot of people did not think she should go." That summer, Chinese-American dissident Harry Wu had been arrested, and relations between the Chinese and United States governments had soured.

"It made people nervous," muses Ginger Lew, who has advised the Obama administration on economics and attended the conference in Beijing. "There was a lot of pressure on her not to go. ... But I don't think there was any question in her mind. She was very clear. She was going." Clinton, Verveer says, "knew that this could make a difference. She wanted to push the envelope on behalf of women and girls around the world, and, throughout that up and down, she just focused on the speech."

"It is time for us to say here in Beijing, and for the world to hear, that it is no longer acceptable to discuss women's rights as separate from human rights," Clinton intoned, 20 years ago this past weekend. In this famous speech, delivered at the United Nations Fourth World Conference on Women on September 5, 1995, Clinton condemned the global injustices that undermined women and girls. But Clinton did not travel to China only to point fingers.

"As an American," she said, "I want to speak up for women in my own country—women who are raising children on the minimum wage, women who can't afford healthcare or childcare, women whose lives are threatened by violence, including violence in their own homes." At the time, Clinton saw that women all over the world were in crisis. She wanted to represent them.

"It is a violation of human rights when babies are denied food, or drowned, or suffocated, or their spines broken, simply because they are born girls," she continued, or "when women and girls are sold into slavery or prostitution for human greed. It is a violation of human rights when women are doused with gasoline, set on fire, and burned to death because their marriage dowries are deemed too small," she said, or "when thousands of women are raped in their own communities and when thousands of women are subjected to rape as a tactic or prize of war."

Her words made a dramatic impression. Clinton, the New York Times *said at the time, had spoken "more forcefully on human rights than any American dignitary has on Chinese soil," including her husband. Looking back, Tina Brown termed it "the speech that launched a movement." As Cecile Richards, President of Planned Parenthood, wrote in an email to Elle.com: "Hillary Clinton helped solidify the idea that human rights are women's rights, and women's rights are human rights." The actress and humanitarian Salma Hayek is still fixated on those immortal words. "It is as if we were considered less than human [until then]," she says. Because of Clinton, she adds, "the eyes of the world were opened to this injustice." Madeline Albright, who also attended the conference, recalls that "without question, Hillary Clinton's speech was the high point of the conference. It was beautifully written and forcefully delivered; it expressed strong support for family values, rapped China for its failure to allow freedom of expression, and highlighted the sentence that would become the hallmark for a global movement."*

"When she uttered those famous words, the place just erupted," Lew states. "In those few words, she…legitimized at the highest level of government around the world that this was an issue that had to be dealt with. The United States was going to be a leader in pushing this agenda, and she was personally vested in this issue."

When it was over, delegates streamed toward Lew to praise the speech: "So many of them rubbed my shoulder or my arm almost as if the magic of the moment could be captured by that." Verveer recalls that "people were on their feet, reaching out to her, screaming as she left the hall. Even delegations that may have been divided in terms of their positions on some of the issues were saying it was a remarkable speech."

- End of excerpts -

Hillary's vision for the children of America is depicted in her book '*It takes a Village*: *And Other Lessons Children Teach Us*' which was published in 1996. The title pretty much covers her message: Our efforts ought to make our society into the kind of village that enables children to flourish. The book was well received in some quarters; it was a *New York Times* best seller. It met fierce criticism from Conservatives.

With Bill Clinton's second term coming to an end in 2000, Hillary sought political office of her own and in January 2001 was sworn in as the junior senator from New York. She was re-elected in 2006 easily.

Hillary Clinton as a U.S. Senator continued with her mission to help children and women.

Hillary authored The Pediatric Research Equity Act in 2003. Former U.S. Senator for Connecticut, Democrat, Chris Dodd expressed Hillary's effort in the following terms: [12]

"Having worked with her in the Senate and on the HELP Committee, the first thing that came to mind was her authorship of the Pediatric Research Equity Act. This law requires drug companies to study their products in children. The Act is responsible for changing the drug labeling of hundreds of drugs with important information about safety and dosing of drugs for children. It has improved the health of millions of children who take medications to treat diseases ranging from HIV to epilepsy to asthma.

Millions of kids are in better shape and alive because of the law Senator Clinton authored."

Hillary Clinton championed the Pay Check Fairness Act and co-sponsored the Lilly Ledbetter Fair Pay Act. For 10 years, Lilly Ledbetter fought to close the gap between women's and men's wages. The Act finally became law when President Obama in January 2009 signed it in to law. [13]

Hillary also fought for legislation to guarantee paid sick leave and paid parental leave for all federal employees.

Two years in to her second term as junior U.S. senator from New York Hillary sought the Democratic Party nomination for president in 2008. She lost the nomination battle to fellow Democratic Senator Barack Obama from Illinois who went on to win the presidency and invited Hillary to be his secretary of state.

As secretary of state Hillary made children's rights and women's rights a cornerstone of U.S. foreign policy.

Race Relations

When we refer to race relations in the United States, at least for now, it's mostly about relationships between Caucasians and African Americans. That would be Whites and Blacks.

There has been no need for a discussion of race relations between Whites and Hispanics. Most Hispanics are also a little white. So, the real Whites are officially referred to as "Non-Hispanic Whites". Mercifully, the only dissatisfaction between Non-Hispanic Whites and Hispanics has been on the subject of immigration.

Donald Trump is trying hard to stirrup animosity between Whites and Hispanics. Trump claims that Hispanics are murdering whites and raping White women. He claims that Hispanics are taking jobs that Whites could otherwise do.

Trump is also trying to create a rift between Blacks and Hispanics. He often says Hispanics take jobs that otherwise Blacks could do.

Unless Trump is stopped in his tracks, soon we will be talking about negative race relations between Whites and Hispanics and also Blacks and Hispanics.

Let me get back to the race relations between Blacks and Whites. What is this all about and how did it all start? I hear on television and talk radio guys and gals speaking eloquently about race relations with absolutely no reference to the history behind this difficult relationship. They either do not have a clue or are choosing to ignore it.

On January 1, 1863, President Abraham Lincoln issued his emancipation proclamation. Slavery ended officially on December 6, 1865 when the 13th Amendment to the constitution was ratified.

African Americans got their right to vote in 1870 under the 15th Amendment. That didn't mean much in some states. They imposed polls taxes and literacy tests as a way of assessing whether anyone was fit or unfit to vote.

Then there were the Civil Rights Acts of 1957 and 1964.

What finally did the trick was the Voting Rights Act of Aug. 6, 1965 of Lyndon Johnson. It outlawed literary tests and poll taxes and all you needed to vote was American citizenship and the registration of your name in an electoral list.[14]

Blacks got the right to vote but not much else in most states, particularly in the southern states.

Martin Luther King Jr. was leading a movement through peaceful protests seeking equality for African Americans.[15]

Race relations in America weren't great when Hillary Clinton was a teenager growing up in Park Ridge, Illinois. She was living with her family. Hillary was a High School freshman when she met Rev. Donald Jones who was leading a Youth Group at the First United Methodist Church of Park Ridge. In 1962 Rev. Jones had taken students from his church including Hillary to hear Rev. Dr. Martin Luther King Jr. preach in Chicago. [16] That apparently was how Hillary got introduced to race relations between Blacks and Whites.

An article by Edward Mcclelland on April 8, 2008 published in Salon.com has an account of how Hillary reacted to the assassination of Martin Luther King. Following are some excerpts: [17]

Forty years and four days ago, Hillary Rodham stormed into a friend's dorm room at Wellesley College and slammed her book bag against a wall.

"I can't stand it anymore!" she screamed, in tears. "I can't take it!"

It was April 4, 1968, and Hillary had just heard the news of Martin Luther King's assassination. The entire nation was grieving that day, but Hillary's anguish was especially palpable, because King himself had started her on her path to political awareness, when she'd shaken his hand after a sermon in Chicago.

The next day, Hillary marched in Boston's Post Office Square, returning to campus wearing a black armband. At a student body meeting at Houghton Memorial Chapel, she boldly spoke in favor of a two-day strike, nearly shouting down a professor who suggested that students give up their weekends instead.

"I'll give up my date Saturday night, Mr. Goldman, but I don't think that's the point," she said. "Individual consciences are fine, but individual consciences have to be made manifest."

- End of excerpts -

It's worth pointing out that Hillary was a 20 year old young white woman from a conservative family at the time Martin Luther King was assassinated.

Rodney Glenn Ellis is the state senator for Texas' 13th state senate district. Following are some excerpts from an article by him titled "Why I'm for Hillary Clinton" published in TribTalk, a publication of the Texas Tribune.[18] Rodney is an African-American, 62 years old and a member of the Democratic Party.

"Even back as a law student in 1972, Hillary traveled around South Texas, going into low-income neighborhoods and registering new African-American and Hispanic voters. She also traveled to Alabama, where she went undercover to investigate and expose school segregation. After law school, she went to South Carolina to find out why so many African-American teenagers were being kept in adult prisons. And a few years later, she opened the first legal aid clinic at the University of Arkansas to help poor families who would not have otherwise had legal assistance.

In the Senate, Hillary sponsored legislation to ban racial profiling, eliminate racial disparities in public health and prosecute hate crimes. And I was glad to see she was a strong supporter of the legislation that eventually became the Matthew Shepard and James Byrd Jr. Hate Crimes Prevention Act. After all, one of my proudest accomplishments in the Texas Senate is sponsoring and passing the James Byrd Jr. Hate Crimes Act — and I couldn't have been more proud of President Obama when he signed the federal law bearing Mr. Byrd's name in 2009.

Hillary Clinton knows that 50 years after the civil rights movement, our country is still filled with too many racial inequalities, where too many black men and women end up in jail, too many minority families lose loved ones to gun violence and too many African-Americans struggle to find jobs that pay a living wage.

That's why she has laid out a "Breaking Every Barrier" agenda — her comprehensive commitment to equity and opportunity in communities of color.

Hillary will bring real, meaningful reform to our broken criminal justice system. She gave her first major speech of the campaign about criminal justice reform, and as president, she'll end the era of mass incarceration, reform mandatory minimum sentences and work to eliminate private prisons. She'll encourage the use of smart strategies like police body cameras, end racial profiling and rebuild trust between law enforcement and the communities they serve. She will also begin to dismantle the school-to-prison pipeline by helping formerly incarcerated individuals successfully re-enter society.

There's a reason Hillary Clinton has been endorsed by Sybrina Fulton, the mother of Trayvon Martin; Gwen Carr, the mother of Eric Garner; Lucia McBath, the mother of Jordan Davis; Marcia Hamilton, the mother of Dontre Hamilton; and Geneva Reed-Veal, the mother of Sandra Bland.

It's because parents across America have seen her show a genuine and lifelong commitment to creating a fairer society."

- End of Expert -

One may choose to agree or disagree on Hillary's views on race relations between Whites and African-Americans. But it's indisputable that Hillary Clinton has from a young age battled for equal opportunity for blacks.

Following are some excerpts from a recent speech by Hillary on race relations:

Excerpts from the transcript of Hillary Clinton's remarks, at Old State Capitol Springfield, Ill., on July 13, 2016:[19]

"President Lincoln led America during the most challenging period in our nation's history. He defended our Union, our Constitution, and the ideal of a nation 'conceived in liberty and dedicated to the proposition that all men are created equal.' His legacy included laws and amendments that enshrined those values for future generations. They protect and guide us still.

Remember, he said, 'A house divided against itself cannot stand. I believe this government cannot endure permanently half slave and half free. I do not expect,' he went on, 'The Union to be dissolved; I do not expect the house to fall. But I do expect it will cease to be divided. It will become all one thing or all the other.'

The challenges we face today do not approach those of Lincoln's time. Not even close. And we should be very clear about that.

But recent events have left people across America asking hard questions about whether we are still a house divided.

Despite our best efforts and highest hopes, America's long struggle with race is far from finished. In just the past week, we saw black men killed by police and five police officers killed by a sniper targeting white police.

There is too much violence and hate in our country. Too little trust and common ground. It can feel impossible to have the conversations we need to have, to fix what's broken.

So I come today as a mother and a grandmother to two beautiful little children. Who, I want them and all our children to grow up in a country where violence like the kind we saw last week doesn't happen again – and where the American Dream is big enough for everyone.

That means taking a hard look at our laws and our attitudes. It means embracing policies that promote justice for all people, and standing firm against any attempt to roll back the clock on the rights and opportunities that so many sacrificed so much to secure.

We do need criminal justice reform to save lives and to make sure all Americans are treated as equals in rights and dignity. We do need to support our police departments that are trying to get it right, and honor the men and women who protect us every day. We do need to do more to stop gun violence. We may disagree about how to do these things, but surely we can all agree with those basic premises. And I hope and pray the past week has showed us how true they are.

I'm running for President with the belief that we need to face up to these challenges and fix them in order to become a stronger, fairer country. And in times like these, we need a President who can help pull us together, not split us apart."

- End of Excerpts –

America elected her first black president, Barack Obama in 2008. In a few decades we will know the long-term influence of his presidency on race relations. As of now, as we are nearing the end of his second term, race relations between Whites and Blacks are not good. Tea Partiers started attacking Obama even before he was sworn in. Donald Trump saw an opportunity in 2011 and grabbed the Birther Movement and we are where we are in the political landscape.

Videos of police officers shooting Black people without apparent justification have stretched race relations to levels we haven't seen for decades. As usual, politicians and media are refusing to see the elephant in the room. The problem between the blacks and the police officers is that they are scared of each other. When a police officer approaches a Black man, the officer is scared for his life. He is scared that the Black man may any minute pull a gun and shoot him. The Black man is equally scared that before this encounter is over, he may get shot by the police officer. I have no solution for this. It's above my pay grade.

All I do know is that we need police officers to protect us and keep peace. They have to find a way to do that without shooting and killing black people for no good reason. Only then, this situation will ease. It is of course a given that nobody, Black, White or Brown has any business killing police officers.

Mr. Trump says he is the 'law and order candidate.' He doesn't appear to see any problem in the Black and White race relations. I say that because he doesn't even talk about it except to say that he is the 'law and order guy.' May be his plan is to order police to shoot as many blacks as necessary to stop them from complaining. That is pretty much in line with his plan to deport 11 million undocumented immigrants to solve the immigration problem. Don't bother with discussing immigration reform, just round them up and kick them out. He has a similar solution for the terrorists' problem. Bomb the shit out of them.

Well, I would go with Hillary on this one.

Immigration

Hillary Clinton's positions on immigration have been consistent over the years. Her opponents have made various claims about Hillary's stands on immigration. When it suites their argument they say Hillary is anti-immigrant. Other times it's claimed that Hillary supports open borders. None of this is true. Basically, throughout her career, the following have been Hillary's positions on immigration:

Hillary is for comprehensive immigration reform including a path to citizenship for undocumented immigrants.

Hillary opposes mass deportation of undocumented immigrants.

Hillary supports deportation of immigrants who are convicted of crimes in the United States. Hillary does not consider a person being in the United States without documents to be a crime to justify deportation.

Hillary maintains that full consideration must be given to the adverse effects on the family members of an undocumented immigrant before breaking up a family and deporting an undocumented immigrant. As a basic principle she opposes breaking up families.

Hillary does not support open borders and is for securing United States' borders by practical means.

Hillary opposes building a wall as promised by Mr. Trump along the southern border. She does not consider it as a suitable and practical way to secure the southern border.

I have read most of the speeches made by Hillary and statements made by her at interviews and at various primary debates on the subject of immigration. The positions stated above are an accurate reflection of her speeches and statements on immigration.

Following are some excerpts of Hillary Clinton's remarks on immigration reform made on May 5, 2015 at Rancho High School, Las Vegas.[20]

"*So we have to do more to make sure that every single child has the best chance to do well in school, to get ahead, to chart his or her own future, to live up to his or her own God given potential. It is also essential that we strengthen families and communities and that means that we have to finally and once and for all fix our immigration system – this is a family issue, its an economic issue too, but it is at heart a family issue. If we claim we are for family then we have to pull together and resolve the outstanding issues around our broken immigration system.*"

"The American people support comprehensive immigration reform not just because it's the right thing to do – and it is – but because it will strengthen families, strengthen our economy, and strengthen our country. That's why we can't wait any longer, we can't wait any longer for a path to full and equal citizenship."

"Now, this is where I differ with everybody on the Republican side."

"Make no mistake: Today not a single Republican candidate, announced or potential, is clearly and consistently supporting a path to citizenship. Not one. When they talk about "legal status," that's code for "second-class status."

"And we should never forget that this debate is about people who, and you're going to meet some of them in a second, people who work hard, who love this country, who pay taxes to it and want nothing more than to build better lives for themselves and their children".

"We're talking about the young people here at this table. They're dreamers in much more than name. They are kids that any parent would be proud of. I don't understand how anyone could look at these kids and think we should break up more families or turn away more hard workers with talent."

"So I will fight for comprehensive immigration reform and a path to citizenship for you and for families across our country. I will fight to stop partisan attacks on the executive actions that would put Dreamers – including many with us today – at risk of deportation."

"And, if Congress refuses to act, as President I will do everything possible under the law to go even further. There are more people – like many parents of Dreamers and others with deep ties and contributions to our communities – who deserve a chance to stay. I'll fight for them too."

"The law currently allows for sympathetic cases to be reviewed, but right now most of these cases have no way to get a real hearing. Therefore we should put in place a simple, straightforward, and accessible way for parents of Dreamers and others with a history of service and contribution to their communities to make their case and be eligible for the same deferred action as their children."

"But that's just the beginning. There's much more to do to expand and enhance protections for families and communities. To reform immigration enforcement and detention practices so they're more humane, more targeted, and more effective. And to keep building the pressure and support for comprehensive reform."

"On a personal basis the first time I ever met anyone who was in our country and working I was about 12 years old, as I recall, and through my church was recruited along with some of the other girls in my Sunday school class to serve as babysitters on Saturday for the small children so that the older children could join their parents in the fields. Because believe it or not when I was growing up in Chicago it was farm fields as far as the eye can see. The immigrant workers would come up through Texas up through the Midwest up to Chicago and then through Michigan and we were asked to help out.

And I remember going out to the camp where the families lived and taking care of the little kids while kids my age were our doing really hard work.

And what stuck in my mind was how at the end of the day, there was a long road at the end of the camp that went out to a dirt road in the middle of the field.

And the bus that had the workers from the field on it that came back in around 4 or 5 o'clock in the afternoon stopped and let the workers off and all these little kids started running down that path to go see their parents and were scooped up by these really really tired people.

And I watched this and just thought, they're just like me and my brothers when my dad comes home from work and we go out there to see him when he comes back from his day of doing what he has to do to support us. I've never gotten that experience or that image out of my mind.

And so for me this is about what kind of people we all are and what kind of country we all have. I am absolutely convinced this is in our economic interest, in the interest of our values and it's even in the interest of our long term security as a nation.

So you know where I stand and there can be no question about it because I will do everything I can as President and during this campaign to make this case.

Now I know there are people who disagree with me and I want them to have a conversation with me.

The facts are really clear, we know how much people who are working hard contribute to our economy both in what they buy and what they pay in taxes. In fact, in NY, which I know a little bit about because I represented it for 8 years and I live there now, our undocumented workers in NY pay more in taxes than some of the biggest corporations in NY. So I'm ready to have this conversation with anyone anywhere.

And now let me turn to those who are living this story I want you to meet them and to talk with them"

- End of Excerpts -

Foreign Policy

The president and the United States Senate are responsible for U.S. foreign policy. The President fashions foreign policy with the approval of the senate. The Department of State is the lead U.S. foreign affairs agency, and the Secretary of State is the President's principal foreign policy adviser. Department of State also supports the foreign affairs activities of other U.S. Government entities such as the Department of Commerce and the U.S. Agency for International Development. [24]

Hillary Clinton was a United States Senator for eight years (2001 to 2009) and a Secretary of State for four years (2009 to 2013). She also served as the First Lady for eight years (1993 to 2001). As Secretary of State Hillary has sat with President Obama in the Situation Room and made her contribution on matters involving life and death of our citizens, our allies and our enemies.

That is why President Obama in his address to the Democratic National Convention in July 2016 described Hillary in the following words: "I can say with confidence there has never been a man or a woman – not me, not Bill, nobody – more qualified than Hillary Clinton to serve as president of the United States of America".[21] ("Bill" he is referring to is Hillary's husband, former president Bill Clinton who was in the audience)

Hillary Clinton has visited 82 countries as First Lady and 112 countries as the Secretary of State. That means a lot. It means personal meetings and friendly relationships with at least 82 heads of state. It also means repetitive personal interactions with secretaries of state or officers at the highest level of at least 112 foreign governments. Why is it a big deal? Because they know firsthand what Hillary Clinton is about and she knows what these leaders are about. That is huge in dealing with nations at a time when most regions in the world are in some form of turmoil.

In January 2009 Hillary Clinton was confirmed as Secretary of State in the full senate by a vote of 94-2.[23]

Iran

The way I see it, the greatest accomplishment by Hillary as Secretary of State is her contribution to avoiding yet another war against yet another Muslim nation, Iran. Israel and some Sunni Arab nations like Saudi Arabia were dead against U.S.A and Iran coming in to any type of agreement on anything. You can't blame them. Iran and these nations are arch enemies. It's in their absolute interest that we too continue to consider Iran as an enemy. They were adamant that Iran should be stopped from getting a nuclear weapon which was our position too. However, these nations, particularly Israel, were not in the least interested in resolving this problem by an agreement between USA and Iran. Bottom line, the alternative was war. A war in the end we had to fight, not them. I could even appreciate that. But I will never be able to understand the opposition by the Republicans and a handful of Democrats for an agreement with Iran that will achieve the objective.

Anyhow, this was the situation that prevailed when Hillary became the Secretary of State. There were some sanctions against Iran which they were coping with. Intelligence made available to American public was that Iran was moving towards getting a nuclear weapon in the not too distant future. Hillary moved in fast. Through sheer diplomacy she was able to get major nations including Russia and China to impose crippling sanctions against Iran which forced them to the negotiating table. As a result, we were able to get an agreement that would prevent Iran from getting a nuclear weapon. Bottom line, we avoided a war.

Could you imagine the United States, right now, involved in a war with Iran with all the other turmoil in the world?

Ceasefire between Israel and Hamas

I also remember watching television news and reading articles about Hillary Clinton brokering a ceasefire between Israel and Hamas in 2012 that ended a war before it escalated out of control. Israel and Hamas has been in violent conflict, off and on, for decades. It's quite true that violence between Israel and Hamas has returned all over again, but it doesn't diminish what Hillary was able to achieve in brokering a ceasefire in 2012. At least that is my humble view. We have had too many wars and conflicts in the recent past and any anyone who helped end one deserves credit.

Libya

Hillary Clinton has been severely criticized for her role in the ouster of Muammar Gaddafi from Libya. The claim by Republicans and others that oppose Hillary is that she was responsible for the Libyan war. This is absolute nonsense. This is not ancient history. Gaddafi's government finally fell in October 2011. That's not even five years ago and it is amazing how some folks try to rewrite such recent history. Fortunately, I do not have to depend on anyone else's account of what happened in Libya five years ago, I closely followed it myself.

The Arab Spring started it. Libyans started to protest which became an uprising. Gaddafi was suppressing the protests by violent police action. There were reports that a lot of Libyan officials were joining the protesters and Gaddafi was losing control of parts of the country. It was around this time that there were reports of a National Transitional Council being formed in Benghazi in the eastern part of Libya. By this time there were horrific reports of Gaddafi's government using brutal force against civilians. It was at this point that Hillary Clinton as the Secretary of State started to play a role in Libyan conflict which was already in an advanced state of a civil war.

France played a prominent role in getting a United Nations Security Council resolution for a no-fly-zone over Libyan airspace. Hillary Clinton gave it her wholehearted backing. Within days there were reports that Libyan army was marching towards Benghazi and some 500,000 civilians would be massacred if nothing was done. It was the French aircrafts that were first to appear on the Libyan sky and I remember CNN newscasters commenting that Americans have surrendered the leading role on this one to the French. It wasn't meant to be a compliment.

This was the origin of the phrase 'Leading from behind' that is so often used by Republicans as a knock on President Obama. Obama is being denigrated for not leading a war that they curse Hillary for promoting. Go figure.

I hate war, but Libya was already in the midst of a horrible civil war. Our closest allies were asking our help to avoid a massacre of huge proportions in their backyard. What do we do?

I would wholeheartedly agree that both President Obama and Secretary Clinton along with their allies failed miserably to do what needed to be done after Gaddafi was deposed. I have heard that the Obama administration expected the Europeans in the Libyan neighborhood to take care of that. It's not even a poor excuse. It's a disgusting excuse.

But don't blame Hillary for going to the aid of our allies and avoiding a massacre of 500,000 Libyans. Hey! The very same Benghazi that she helped to save has come back to haunt her in no small measure. That is what happens sometimes in world diplomacy. I haven't heard her complaining even once.

Gay rights

Standing up for minority rights has been one of Hillary's things and it doesn't surprise me in the least that in her capacity as Secretary of State she wanted to advance the rights of a community that is yet to be treated fairly in most parts of the world. She lobbied for the first-ever U.N. Human Rights Council resolution on human rights and declared that "gay rights are human rights."

U.S. position in the world

Above all, I believe that Hillary's greatest accomplishment as our top diplomat was also the hardest to achieve. I take no pleasure in saying this. But facts are stubborn. By the end of the second term of George W. Bush's presidency, the reputation of the United States in the world was in the pits. Bottom line, we dragged so many of our allies and friends in to Iraq in search of so called 'Weapons of mass destruction' which were never there in the first place. We not only embarrassed them, so many of their finest paid the ultimate sacrifice. Tens of thousands of Iraqis lost their lives and millions more were displaced. We lost thousands of our finest with additional tens of thousands injured which would only have added to the misery of our allies and friends. It was sad and ugly and it didn't help that at the same time most of the economies in the world were either in a recession or entering one.

That was our reputation in the world when Hillary took over as our top diplomat. As Secretary of State she was the key in rebuilding America's leadership and prestige overseas. She restored our alliances with the EU and key Asian allies as well as key relationships in Africa and Latin America. America's reputation in the world was as good as, or better than it ever has been, when Hillary handed over the baton to her successor John Kerry.

Republicans say that America's standing in the world was at its best when Obama took over from Bush and it's at its worst as he is finishing his second term. I am not surprised. These are the guys who are fighting to have Trump as their next president.

National Security

Following are excerpts from the Fact Sheet: The 2015 National Security Strategy of the White House.[25]

"We will advance the security of the United States, its citizens, and U.S. allies and partners by:

Maintaining a national defense that is the best trained, equipped, and led force in the world while honoring our promises to service members, veterans, and their families.

Working with Congress to end the draconian cuts imposed by sequestration that threaten the effectiveness of our military and other instruments of power.

Reinforcing our homeland security to keep the American people safe from terrorist attacks and natural hazards while strengthening our national resilience.

Transitioning to a sustainable global security posture that combines our decisive capabilities with local partners and keeps pressure on al-Qa'ida, ISIL, and their affiliates.

Striving for a world without nuclear weapons and ensuring nuclear materials do not fall into the hands of irresponsible states and violent non-state actors.

Developing a global capacity to prevent, detect, and rapidly respond to biological threats like Ebola through the Global Health Security Agenda.

Confronting the urgent crisis of climate change, including through national emissions reductions, international diplomacy, and our commitment to the Green Climate Fund."

- End of excerpts -

The fact sheet continues to describe the means that will be adopted to do what is necessary.

If Hillary Clinton were to be elected president, she will also set forth a strong National Security Strategy of her own.

If Mr. Trump were to be elected president, I have no idea what he would do. This is not to slight him. I am just being honest.

A president's primary duty is to keep our nation safe from enemies foreign and domestic. Very briefly, to do so he or she needs a strong economy at home and a strong military. From where we are today, we have every reason to believe that when President Obama leaves office in January 2017, he will leave behind a good enough economy and a military second to none in the world.

Hillary Clinton has the experience and the knowhow to keep us safe. I'll give just one example to show why I am so confident.

At one of Hillary's Town Hall meetings during her primary contest with Bernie Sanders, one of the participants asked her a question on national security. I witnessed it on television. An account of it was published by Gabby Morrongiello on 2/3/2016 in Washington Examiner.[26] Following are excerpts from her article:

DERRY, N.H. -- Hillary Clinton fielded a tough question during CNN's Democratic Presidential Town Hall Wednesday evening from an undecided Democratic voter who worried about her hawkish foreign policy instincts.

"As a senator and as Secretary of State, you have a history of interventionist foreign policy that is troubling to many Democratic voters, including myself," a young man named Michael, who was identified as leaning towards supporting Clinton's opponent, Vermont Sen. Bernie Sanders, told the former first lady. "As a voter who is opposed to the U.S. being the world's policemen, can you assure me that, as president, you would not expand our military involvement abroad?"

"No I can't, Michael," Clinton was quick to respond.

"I mean, I'd like to be able to say I could, but here's what I can say," she quickly followed up. "I have learned, and really been in the crucible of making a lot hard decisions over the last years, [that] military force must always be a last resort not a first choice."

"I worked very hard as Secretary of State to do what I could diplomatically to avoid conflict," Clinton said. "That's why I worked to put the coalition together to impose sanctions on Iran so we could get them to the negotiating table in order to test whether we could get an agreement to put a nuclear weapons agreement in place."

She continued, "I will do everything I possibly can to avoid sending American troops abroad and getting us involved in military conflicts, but I can't in good conscience tell you that there would never be any circumstances in the time I served as president where it very well might be in America's best, vital national security interest."

While declining to rule out taking any military action if she makes it to the Oval Office, Clinton said she would "not send American combat troops to Iraq or Syria" and claimed that doing so before was "an awful mistake."

"I will be a very careful, deliberate decision-maker when facing hard choices because I know what is at stake," she said. "I know you can understand why there can't be, from me anyway, a blanket statement, but I want to assure you, I will be transparent, I will be open and I will explain to the

*American people if any occasion arises where we do
have to take military action to protect ourselves or
our close friends or partners."*

- End of Excerpts -

Hillary's vote for the Iraq war has dogged her twice
in her bid for the presidency of the United States.
Then Senator Obama hammered her persistently on
it in 2008. It obviously contributed for her losing that
primary to Obama.

In this year's (2016) primary, Senator Sanders went
after her on this same issue as aggressively as
Senator Obama did in 2008. On the day that this
town hall was being held in New Hampshire, Hillary
was losing in New Hampshire to Bernie 55 to 38 in
the latest Real Clear Polls average.

That's the background in which we have to consider
Michael's question and Hillary's answer. She didn't
hesitate for one second before answering the
question.

I am no hawk. I hate war. But I also do not want to
be run over by a dictator large or small.

Osama Bin Laden

Hillary argued for going after Osama Bin Laden
when she knew very well that the stakes were so
high for the Obama administration of which she was
an integral part.

That shows strength to do the right thing irrespective

of possible disastrous consequences to one's self interest.

Will keep us safe

Hillary's actions as a U.S. Senator and as the Secretary of State is irrefutable testimony that she will further strengthen our Military and keep the NATO alliance and our other alliances with friendly nations strong.

I am more than satisfied that Hillary Clinton is presidential material and that she will keep my family and this nation strong and safe.

Economy

Hillary Clinton had a front row seat as the first lady during her husband Bill Clinton's two terms as president. Actually it was more than a front row seat; unlike most other former first ladies, Hillary was directly involved in Bill Clinton administration. Our economy flourished during Bill's two terms and Hillary had the opportunity to observe and support the policies that were implemented and worked so well.

Hillary was a U.S. Senator from New York, the financial capital of the world, during George W. Bush's two terms as president. She had an obligation to study, observe and support or oppose Bush's economic policies. Not even Republicans will deny that she fulfilled this obligation with distinction. Thus, she saw the disastrous consequences of Bush's massive tax-cuts to the rich and the

Republican's obsession with de-regulation. It was evident that the so called 'trickle-down economics' and irresponsible de-regulation didn't work. Hillary vehemently opposed Bush's economic policies that led the nation to the worst recession since the Great Depression.

Hillary was the Secretary of State during the first term of the Obama presidency. She was a major player in the Obama administration that prevented the country from sliding in to a depression. She was a party to the successful economic policies of the Obama administration that dug the nation out of the Great Recession. Those economic policies have reduced the unemployment rate by almost half of what it was when Obama took office and have created more than 14 million private sector jobs since the lowest point during the Great Recession.

Nevertheless, too many Americans have lost their good paying jobs because the companies they worked for have moved their manufacturing to foreign lands, mostly to take advantage of cheap labor. Another huge cause for loss of good jobs is automation. Walk in to any bank and observe how many of the senior staff and tellers have disappeared. Make a telephone call to any company, corporation, federal, state, or city office. You will be lucky if you get to talk to a human being. Globalization, trade agreements and automation have its positives and negatives. The positives are of no consolation to a family where the breadwinner has lost a decent good paying job for no fault of his and the new job he could find can barely put food on the table. Those high paying jobs are not coming back, and to promise otherwise is cruel and dishonest. Free training for good paying jobs that global economy is producing and simultaneously providing supplemental benefits to those families is the only decent thing do.

Hillary has the heart to work for an economy that will benefit the middle-class and the poor. The economic framework that her campaign has put forth so far is to that end. Main proposals include raising the minimum wage, and a much needed massive infrastructure program that will necessarily provide good paying jobs. Hillary has been around long enough to find brilliant economists to do the job.

Hillary's idea of a good economy is one that would enable all people to get rich. That is the American way. She has absolutely no problem with rich Americans getting richer as long as they don't do so at the expense of the middle class and the poor. Hillary also is a firm believer that the rich need to make their fair contribution to maintain and improve the society in which they live in so comfortably. The rich are quick to point out deficiencies of the federal government, but when it comes to paying their fair share of taxes they do so grudgingly. Most of them (not all) make use of every possible loophole to avoid paying taxes. That isn't going to cut with Hillary Clinton if she were to be the next president. As her campaign progresses during the remaining twelve weeks she will layout her goals with more clarity and the plan to achieve them.

Education

If you support public education, Hillary is your woman. That's what she has done throughout her long career.

Hillary has also always been a strong advocate for educators.

Hillary has always supported early childhood education.

Whenever Title 1, the federal program providing funding for local school districts to improve the academic achievement of disadvantaged students, had to be reauthorized, Hillary was there fighting big for its reauthorization.

Hillary has no problem with charter schools as long as they are not for profit. But she does recognize that most charter schools don't work with the most challenging students. Public schools on the other hand take care of every child's education and Hillary is adamant that they get the resources and support they need.

A high school certificate isn't sufficient anymore to find a decent job. A two year community college degree is more or less a minimum requirement. A four year college degree has become the norm for a good paying job. College, though, has become very expensive.

Higher education and burdensome student debt has gone hand in hand for far too long. Difficulty in finding good paying jobs after graduation has made the burden heavier. Those who need help with their 'student debt' need realistic relief. Likewise, measures have to be put in place to prevent future graduates from finding themselves in the same untenable position.

Hillary Clinton's campaign has been working on these issues. Current proposals include finding a way to provide free community college education for all students. They are also working to provide debt-free four year college to students whose parents' annual income is below a certain amount. I believe the figure being discussed is around $125,000.00. Proposals are also being considered to provide relief for those who are already burdened with large amounts of student debt. Irrespective of who wins the presidency, these measures are necessary for our young to have a chance at the American dream. These proposals need funding. Adding to the national debt is not a viable option. I am confident that Hillary's economists will find a way.

Healthcare

Nobody has fought harder than the late senator from Massachusetts Ted Kennedy and Hillary Clinton to get universal healthcare to all Americans.

Hillary tried it in 1993 when she was First Lady. The plan was officially known as the 'Health Security Act" and detractors called it 'Hillarycare'. Republicans and health insurance industry killed it. It is also generally believed that the effort also cost the Democrats the majority in the House of Representatives in 1994.

In 1997 Hillary as First Lady helped the late-Senator Ted Kennedy, a Massachusetts' Democrat and

Republican Senator Orrin Hatch from Utah to get a health insurance program for children enacted. It's the Children's Health Insurance Program known as CHIP and now provides health insurance to over 8 million children.

After several attempts by successive Democratic administrations, finally in 2009, President Obama was able to get the landmark legislation 'The Affordable Care Act' enacted which has so far provided health insurance to 22 million Americans. Had all Republican state legislatures and Republican governors cooperated in implementing the Affordable Care Act, many more millions would now have health insurance. Unfortunately, they not only refused to cooperate, but also went out of their way to obstruct the implementation of the Act. So did successive U.S. Houses of Representatives controlled by Republicans. They challenged vital components of the Act all the way to the Supreme Court on more than one occasion. Each of those challenges was flatly rejected by the court. Republican controlled Houses on more than fifty occasions passed legislation to repeal the Health Care Act or some part of it.

Trump is promising to repeal the Affordable Care Act within the first 100 days, if he were to be elected president. Hillary is promising to expand the Act to cover all Americans. One of the measures she is considering to achieve that objective is to provide for a 'public option' in the Act.

It's not an exaggeration to state that the health insurance of millions of Americans is in the balance in the upcoming presidential election.

The Trust Issue

"For the great enemy of the truth is very often not the lie - deliberate, contrived and dishonest - but the myth, persistent, persuasive, and unrealistic." [27]

John F. Kennedy

I dare hope that by now I have made a solid case for Hillary Clinton to be the next president of the United States based on her experience and past actions.

However, some of you may still have lingering questions on the so called 'Trust issue' that has plagued Hillary during this campaign.

A long time ago in January 1993, Hillary Clinton entered the White House as America's First Lady. A catch phrase during her husband Bill Clinton's 1992 presidential campaign was that, if he were to be elected president, Americans will get 'Two for the price of one', the 'two' being Bill and Hillary. By then, she had been Arkansas' First Lady for 12 years and her stands on race relations and children's issues have made Hillary a rising Liberal star.

Republicans were still recovering from the shock of Bill Clinton winning the presidency. It didn't take long for them to notice another emerging threat. First Lady Hillary Clinton, an unusually strong woman terrified them. They were going to do something about it and they did.

Allegations against Hillary that were proved to be

totally false were nevertheless pushed persistently and persuasively until they became myths. Liberals had a name for this sustained, brutal effort by the Republicans. They called it "Conspiracy theories".

Let me name a few and before doing so make it absolutely clear that these allegations have been examined by one or more authoritative bodies namely, U.S. congress, U.S. justice department, FBI, and independent counsel and found to be false. Also please bear in mind that the Republicans meant to damage both Hillary and Bill and an allegation against one was meant to tarnish both. It was always 'Clintons' not one or the other. Wherever possible, they also tried to associate the Democratic Party with the so called scandals.

Filegate

You still hear Republicans and Conservatives trying to demonize Hillary and Bill over what came to be known as 'Filegate'.

It started during the first term of Bill Clinton's presidency. The allegations were that First lady Hillary Clinton and some other members of the White House staff illegally obtained FBI files of some Republicans. Also, that Hillary improperly hired Craig Livingstone, the director of the White House's office of personal security.

The matter was investigated by the House Government Reform and Oversight Committee, Senate Judiciary Committee, and independent counsels Kenneth Starr and Robert Ray.

In 1998, Kenneth Starr exonerated President Clinton and First Lady Hillary Clinton of any involvement in the matter.

In 2000, Robert Ray issued his final report on filegate stating *"There is no credible evidence that senior White House figures or Mrs. Clinton had requested the files or had acted improperly or testified improperly regarding Livingstone's hiring."*

A separate lawsuit on the matter brought by Judicial Watch, a Conservative watch dog group lingered on and was dismissed by a federal judge in 2010.

Let's look at what happened here. A serious but false allegation was brought against the Clintons in the third year of the first term of Bill Clinton's presidency. It was headline news in all major news papers and prime time TV. Hillary was called a criminal. The sarcasm against the Clintons was brutal. Republicans and Conservatives kept the story alive for years. The fact that it was a lie didn't matter. They continued to push a narrative that Clintons were above the law and cannot be trusted. Bill was, and still is a charming personality and is considered to have been an excellent president. The majority of Americans still love him. This bugged his opposition to no end. Hillary on the other hand was a much easier target. Forgive me for saying this, even as late as the nineties, most Americans, including women, didn't care too much for strong women. It was like there was something wrong with them. It was easy to keep a false narrative alive that 'Hillary must have done something wrong.' The media loved it. This was about the First Lady, a sensational story. The so called Liberal media pushed it as hard as the Conservative channels. It got to a point that the mention of the word 'Filegate' was enough to bring negative thoughts about Hillary Clinton. This went on for two decades and still goes on.

Whitewater

This was about a real estate investment by Bill and Hillary Clinton in the Whitewater Development Corporation, a failed business venture in the 1970s and 1980s. Clintons actually lost money on this venture. The allegation was that Bill Clinton, when he was governor of Arkansas put pressure on a banker to make a loan to Bill and Hillary's associates in Whitewater Corporation, Jim and Susan McDougal. The Clintons were never prosecuted for anything to do with Whitewater but became targets of several Whitewater inquiries during Bill's two terms as president.

United States Senate and United States House conducted inquiries and held hearings on Whitewater. At Clintons' request Attorney General Janet Reno appointed a special prosecutor, Robert B. Fiske, to investigate the legality of the Whitewater transactions. Fiske was replaced by Kenneth Starr to continue the investigation.

Hillary Clinton testified before a grand jury concerning her investments in Whitewater. This was the first time in American history that a first lady had been subpoenaed to testify before a grand jury. She testified that they never borrowed any money from the bank, and denied having caused anyone to borrow money on their behalf.

Then there was a Special White Water Committee. Its hearings ran for 300 hours over 60 sessions across 13 months, and taking over 10,000 pages of testimony and 35,000 pages of depositions from almost 250 people. The investigation mostly followed on partisan lines. Republicans were in the majority. The Senate Special Whitewater Committee issued an 800-page majority report which only hinted at one possible improper action by President Clinton. Hillary Clinton was referred to as "the central figure" in the alleged wrong doings.

After all the hearings including a grand jury hearing and investigations lasting over five years, it amounted to, *'a hint at a possible improper action by Bill Clinton.'*

The Democratic minority on the Committee called the hearings and investigations "a legislative travesty," "a witch-hunt," and "a political game."

So my friends, that was another attempt by the Republicans and Conservatives to bring down the Clintons. It failed because the allegations had no merit, but they achieved their objective of dragging Clintons in mud for years and years over this and haven't stopped yet. All news media including the so called "liberal media" had years of fun with this. Speak of sensational news – a First Lady, for the first time in American history, testifying before a grand jury. You cannot make this stuff up.

Death of Vince Foster in 1993

Vince Foster was a partner at Rose Law Firm in Arkansas and was a friend and college of Hillary Clinton who was also a partner at Rose before becoming America's First Lady.

When Bill Clinton became president in January 1993 Foster joined the White House staff as Deputy White House Counsel.

In July 1993 he was found dead in a federal park in Virginia, outside Washington D.C.

His death was determined to have been a suicide by six official investigations. That meant nothing to some Conservatives who were enemies of Clintons. They spread rumors that Bill and Hillary Clinton were somehow involved in the death of Vince Foster.

The investigations were by U.S. Park police, Department of Justice, FBI, Independent Counsel Robert B. Fiske and Independent Counsel Kenneth Starr. They all concluded that Fosters death was a suicide.

United States Congress also held hearings to determine whether the White House was guilty of improper conduct during the course of the park service police investigation into the death.

After a three year investigation, Kenneth Starr concluded that Foster's death was a suicide.

CNN carried a story on July 15, 1997 on Kenneth Starr's report.[30] After having reported Starr's conclusion, the story added, "A determined band of conspiracy theorists postulated that Foster, who had intimate knowledge of the Clintons' affairs, was murdered because he knew too much. Starr's report throws more cold water on that thesis." It went further to include: "Starr's ruling may put to rest speculation that Foster, a longtime Arkansas associate of Bill and Hillary Clinton, was murdered."

That was wishful thinking. The investigation reports didn't mean anything to right-wing political groups.

Folks, they were alleging that a sitting president of the United States and his First Lady murdered a member of their staff and covered it up. Go figure. They haven't given up and still push this story today.

Allegations against the President and the First Lady continued during the entirety of Bill's two terms. Travelgate, Chinagate, IRS gate, Iranian fund raising and on and on they continued.

Not a single allegation against Hillary Clinton was proved because they were all false.

The allegation against Bill Clinton over the Lewinski affair was proved because it was true and he paid a heavy price for it and so did Hillary and Chelsea.

As President Bill Clinton was ending his second term, Republicans, Conservatives and Right-wingers had plenty to celebrate. Not only were Bill and Hillary leaving the White House, their guy George W. Bush was coming in.

Hillary's election as the junior senator from New York was a spoiler, but only a minor distraction compared to Bush's victory.

The fun didn't last too long though. Soon they had to contend with 9-11 followed by Bush's two wars.

Then there was a congressional election followed by a presidential election in which John Kerry gave a run for his money to Bush. That was followed by another congressional election in which the GOP lost the majority in the Senate.

Then it was the bursting of the housing bubble, financial collapse and the Great Recession.

Republicans, Conservatives and Right-wingers were busy providing cover for Bush's misdeeds and the Clintons had a well deserved respite from their ugly attacks.

2007/2008 Democratic presidential primary took the GOP by surprise. Democrats were going to have either a woman or a black man as their nominee. How could this possibly be? After the initial shock, they settled down and went to work. For Obama it was Rev. Jeremiah Wright and for Hillary the old allegations were back in circulation.

When Obama won the nomination, they stopped going after Hillary.

Then, when Obama won the presidency, he brought Hillary in as his Secretary of State. Republicans, Conservatives and Right-wingers couldn't believe it. It was like this woman keeps popping up like a bad coin. For Democrats, Hillary was their rising Liberal star next to Obama.

President Obama was a handful for the Republicans and Tea-Partiers. They were totally pre-occupied with obstructing him and trying to bring him down, and more or less left Hillary alone.

That was only until Hillary resigned as Secretary of State. I believe Republicans were convinced that Hillary would run for president in 2016, even before she knew for sure that she would. It didn't take long for them to start on her all over again. It's like a game for them. All the old false allegations are back in circulation.

Hardly a day passes without a Fox News talk show host mentioning Filegate or some other gate. Talk radio rumbles with all the gates.

None in the main street media likes Hillary. The so called Liberal media is no exception. They have helped demonize her for a quarter century.

The forces that oppose Hillary are smart. They know that rehashing old allegations isn't going to be enough to defeat her. So they have manufactured a few new ones. "Benghazi" is one. Another is "Hillary is responsible for Libya." They are looking for some scandal to associate with "Clinton Foundation." And Hillary gave them a gift, "The email controversy."

We have already covered Libya. Let's look in to Benghazi and the email controversy.

Benghazi

What happened at Benghazi was a tragedy. U.S. Ambassador Christopher Stevens and three other

U.S. nationals were killed in an attack that happened on September 11, 2012 at the U.S. mission in Benghazi, Libya and at an annex in a nearby compound.

A presidential election was to be held in USA on November 6, 2012. The degree to which partisan politics associated with that election influenced the various enquiries into this tragedy is pretty disturbing.

Within 24 hours of the first report of the attack, Republican presidential candidate Mitt Romney released a statement condemning the Obama administration for the tragedy. His statement didn't make any sense.[32]

Republicans weren't concerned with what happened to four Americans who perished while serving this nation in a foreign land. They were hell bent on using the tragedy for their political advantage. You have read how they tried to harm the Clintons by making something out of nothing. You have read what they did with the death of Vince Foster. This was no different.

The day these Americans were killed there were protests in some Muslim countries because of a YouTube video released by an American. The video contained material defamatory of Prophet Muhammad.

Initial reports by the White House and the Department of State indicated that the attacks in Benghazi started as protests against the video; that the protests turned in to violent riots that killed the four Americans. It was subsequently established that the attack on the Mission was a terrorist attack.

You may find this hard to believe, but the entire Benghazi controversy started over the contention that the White House and the State Department tried to attribute the Benghazi attacks to the YouTube video, because, if the Benghazi attack was seen to be a terrorist attack, it would contradict the White House contention that the terrorists are on the run. That it would then damage President Obama's chances of re-election. The whole story is contorted. You have to hand it to Republicans for making something out of nothing. You have read how good they have been at that in attacking the Clintons.

The accusations were expanded to allege that the Obama administration delayed sending a CIA rescue team and failed to try a military rescue.

There have been at least eight congressional investigations in to the Benghazi attacks. In addition there have been investigations by the FBI, the State Department and others.

Following are excerpts from an article by Jon ponder in Pensito Review published on November 25, 2014 depicting findings of the seventh congressional investigation: [33]

The CIA and the military acted properly in responding to the 2012 attack on a U.S. diplomatic compound in Benghazi, Libya, a Republican-controlled House committee has found. Its report concluded that there was no wrongdoing by Obama administration officials.

Debunking a series of persistent allegations hinting at dark conspiracies, the two-year investigation of the politically charged incident determined that there was no intelligence failure, no delay in sending a CIA rescue team, no missed opportunity for a military rescue, and no evidence the CIA was covertly shipping arms from Libya to Syria.

Immediately after the attack, intelligence about who carried it out and why was contradictory, the report found. That led Susan Rice, then U.S. ambassador to the United Nations, to inaccurately assert that the attack had evolved from a protest, when in fact there had been no protest.

But it was intelligence analysis, not political appointees, who made the wrong call, the committee found. The report did not conclude that Rice or any other government official acted in bad faith or intentionally misled the American people.

– End of excerpts -

The above were findings of a Republican controlled House Committee. But the Republicans wouldn't let Benghazi go away. Oh no! President Obama got re-elected, but Hillary Clinton is in the wings preparing for the 2016 presidential election. There is no way that the GOP would let Benghazi go before inflicting whatever possible damage it can on Hillary. After all, Hillary was the head of the department of state when Benghazi happened. Hillary had already taken responsibility as the Secretary of State for the inadequate security at the Mission when the attack took place.

So we had the eighth investigation by yet another Republican controlled select committee.

Two Republicans spilled the beans on what this investigation was all about. Of course it was about hurting Mrs. Clinton and her campaign for president.

California Congressman House Majority leader Kevin McCarthy was one of the two congressmen who dropped the ball. Following is an account of how it happened as described in a Washington Post article by Chris Cillizza on September 30, 2015: [34]

House Republicans are in the midst of a coronation of California Congressman Kevin McCarthy as the next Speaker of the House. McCarthy's comments about the motives of the House select committee investigating the attacks in Benghazi, Libya, on Tuesday night, however, should give the party pause about whether he's totally ready for the big job.

Prodded repeatedly by Conservative Fox News Channel host Sean Hannity to name an accomplishment for the Republican-led Congress, McCarthy seized on the Benghazi committee and its investigation into Hillary Clinton's role (or lack thereof) in the handling of the incident during her time as Secretary of State.

"Everybody thought Hillary Clinton was unbeatable, right?" McCarthy told Hannity. "But we put together a Benghazi special committee, a select committee. What are her numbers today? Her numbers are dropping. Why? Because she's untrustable. But no

one would have known any of that had happened, had we not fought."

Whoops!

- End of Excerpts –

The other congressman to shoot his mouth off was New York Republican Rep. Richard Hanna. His comments are described in an article published in The Washington Post by Chris Cillizza on October 15, 2015: [35] Following are some excerpts:

Hillary Rodham Clinton won't appear before the House select committee tasked with investigating the deaths of four Americans in Benghazi, Libya, until next Thursday. But, thanks to House Republicans, she's already got a major leg up, politically speaking.

First came House Majority Leader Kevin McCarthy's career-killing comment that the Benghazi committee deserved credit for dragging down Clinton's poll numbers. Now we have Rep. Richard Hanna (N.Y.) who told a local radio station this week that "this may not be politically correct, but I think that there was a big part of this investigation that was designed to go after people and an individual, Hillary Clinton." Hanna added: "I think that's the way Washington works. But you'd like to expect more from a committee that's spent millions of dollars and tons of time."

Oomph. While McCarthy's comments were the sort of thing where, in the most positive light, you could see them being something short of an indictment of the roots and goals of the Benghazi committee, Hanna's are not. This is a politically motivated operation aimed at trying to damage the leading Democratic candidate for president, according to Hanna. Not much room for misunderstanding there.

- End of Excerpt -

Well, they held the hearing and Republicans grilled Hillary Clinton for nearly 11 hours and couldn't lay a finger on her. The spectacle is adequately described in an article by contact reporters Evan Harper and David Lauter published on October 22, 2015.in Los Angeles Times. Following are a few excerpts: [36]

Republicans grilled former Secretary of State Hillary Rodham Clinton through nearly 11 hours Thursday in a long-awaited hearing of the House Benghazi committee that produced little if any new information, but ample partisan argument.

The hearing provided an extraordinary spectacle, starting in the morning and stretching well into the night, far longer than such sessions typically last even with multiple witnesses.

Through the lengthy session, Clinton maintained a relentlessly calm and smiling demeanor, showing few visible signs of fatigue other than a hoarse throat that began to develop in the 10th hour.

From her opening statement on, she sought to seize a rhetorical high ground above the partisan fray, reminding members of the panel that after attacks on diplomatic facilities during the administrations of Ronald Reagan, Bill Clinton and George W. Bush in

which hundreds of Americans were killed, members of both parties "rose above politics" to examine what had gone wrong.
- End of Excerpt –

The investigation produced no new information. At least for now, the investigations appear to have come to an end, but just as with every previous false allegation against her, the GOP effort to tarnish Hillary over Benghazi continues.

Email controversy

Hillary Clinton, when she was Secretary of State has used her private email account maintained on her family server for official communications. She could have saved herself a lot of heartache had she used official state department email accounts maintained on federal servers.

Hillary admitted that it was a mistake and has apologized for it. We have seen what her opponents have done to bring her down when she had made no mistakes. While an apology was necessary and the right thing to do, it made no difference to her opponents. They went after her on this with a vengeance. They claimed that she broke the law and should be locked up.

Hillary maintained from the beginning and up to this date that she didn't receive or send any emails marked "Classified" on her private email account. When it came to be known that some of those emails have been classified retroactively, an FBI investigation was initiated regarding how classified information was handled on Clinton's private server.

James Comey, the director of FBI who conducted the investigation filed his concluding report on July 5, 2016.

He found that nearly 2100 emails on the server have been retroactively marked classified.

That 113 emails contained information that was classified at the time it was sent. That 65 of the 113 deemed "Secret" and 22 deemed "Top Secret."

That out of the 113 emails, only 3 contained markings that they could be classified, That even in those 3, there were no "Classified headers," but only had a © marking. The state department had said subsequently that even those © markings were there by a mistake at the state department. In any event, Mr. Comey had said that Secretary Clinton may not have known that the © marking meant that they could contain classified information.

Mr. Comey concluded that Hillary Clinton had not broken any laws but had been very careless in using a private email account and server.

So, the bottom line is that when Hillary said that she did not receive or send documents marked "Classified," she was telling the truth. However, that will not do her a fat lot of good. It isn't possible to explain these details to millions of voters. The more she tries, the worse it will sound. It will sound like she is trying to cover up some wrong doing. Her opponents will use this against her for the rest of the campaign. That is something she will have to live with.

Standing by your man

Is standing by your man a terrible thing to do?

Biographers and many others have written much about Hillary and Bill. I have read a lot of those accounts and they all have relied on information they received from others who have been close to the Clintons in one capacity or the other.

Well, I have followed the Clintons closely from the time of Bill's first campaign to the White House. That was in 1991/1992. I followed them on TV and through reports in newspapers and magazines. It has been over a long period of time and what I heard them say and saw how they interacted is what I heard and saw firsthand. I prefer to believe that rather than what others have written second or third hand, some of which has been very supportive of the Clintons and some very negative.

I observed a couple who were attached to each other, needed each other and depended on each other. They surely were also very fond of each other. I obviously couldn't get into Hillary's head to read her thoughts, but every time I saw them together it was apparent that Hillary considered Bill to belong to her. That is what I observed through their good times and rough patches. The ugly times were mostly at the hands of Conservatives and Right wingers.

I remember as if yesterday, the look on Hillary's face as she was leaving the White House to go on their so called vacation after the Monica Lewinski affair.

Hillary was holding Chelsea in one hand. Bill was walking a little away from them. The pain, shame, anger, and disbelief on her face were painful to watch. Chelsea was a teenager and looked confused and distracted. These are human beings just like any one of us.

Hillary obviously valued marriage and a home for her daughter with both parents around. And she wanted her man. But the way she was vilified for that was astonishing. They cursed her, ridiculed her and laughed at her for not walking away from her marriage.

Well, they are still together; and Chelsea has turned out to be an exemplary young woman. I wish them well, maybe you will too.

She is still standing

The effort by Republicans, Conservatives and Right wingers to vilify Hillary Clinton was vast. What I have described in this chapter is only a fraction of their effort.

Of all the allegations leveled against her, only two have some merit and Hillary has taken responsibility for both.

There ought to have been better security at the temporary consulate in Benghazi and the ultimate responsibility for such matters lie squarely with the secretary of state. Hillary has taken responsibility for that.

Hillary should have used the email accounts and servers of the Department of State for her official communications and not her personal email account and server. She has admitted that what she did was a mistake.

All other allegations against Hillary from the day she entered the White House as First Lady in January 1993 have been proved to be false by multiple official entities that investigate them, often multiple times. That obviously made no difference to her accusers who manufactured the allegations.

Sensational stories sell newspapers and attract Television viewers and radio audiences. Media has helped her opponents to keep these stories alive.

Hillary Clinton has weathered this ugly campaign against her for almost a quarter century and is still standing.

New Yorkers trusted Hillary twice by huge margins to represent them as their United States senator.

After a hard fought and close primary against her in 2008, President Obama trusted Hillary to be his Secretary of State.

Democrats have opted to trust her to be their nominee for president in a primary race against a thoroughly trusted and eminently decent senator called Bernie Sanders from Vermont.

The only trust issue that Hillary has is what had been manufactured by Republicans, Conservatives and Right wingers for over 23 years.

I am confident that on November 8th 2016 the vast majority of Americans will place their trust in Hillary Clinton to be their president.

The Truth will prevail over the Myth.

NOTES

Chapter 1: Presidency of George W. Bush

1. United States Department of Labor, Bureau of labor Statistics – TED: The Economics Daily. Unemployment Rate Rises In January, February 05, 2001. United States Department of Labor http://www.bls.gov/opub/ted/2001/feb/wk1/art01.htm

2. United States Department of Labor, Bureau of labor Statistics – TED: The   Economics Daily. Increase in unemployment rate in January 2009, February 10, 2009. United States Department of Labor http://www.bls.gov/opub/ted/2009/feb/wk2/art02.htm

3. *The* National Bureau *of* Economic Research. Business Cycle Dating Committee, National Bureau of Economic Research. Determination of the December 2007 Peak in Economic Activity. *the* National Bureau of Economic Research http://www.nber.org/cycles/dec2008.html

4. CNN Money. SPECIAL REPORT Issue #1: America's Money Crisis. Bailout is law. President Bush signs historic $700 billion plan aimed at stemming credit crisis. By Jeanne Sahadi, CNNMoney.com senior writer, Last Updated: October 4, 2008. CNN Money http://money.cnn.com/2008/10/03/news/economy/house_friday_bailout/

5. Eye on the Economy on NBCNEWS.com. Study: 1.2 million households lost to recession. By John W. Schoen, Senior producer, MSNBC.com, updated 4/8/2010 NBCNews.com

6. THE WHITE HOUSE, The Lowest Unemployment Rate in 30 Years. Office of the Press Secretary, For Immediate Release, January 7, 2000. THE CLINTON-GORE ECONOMIC RECORD: THE LOWEST UNEMPLOYMENT RATE IN 30 YEARS. THE WHITE HOUSE http://clinton4.nara.gov/WH/New/html/20000112_1.html

[Note: This is historical material, "frozen in time." The website is no longer updated and links to external websites and some internal pages will not work]

7. The WHITE HOUSE. PRESIDENT GEORGE W. BUSH. BUSH RECORD. President Bush Helped Americans Through Tax Relief. The WHITE HOUSE https://georgewbush-whitehouse.archives.gov/infocus/bushrecord/factsheets/taxrelief.html
[Note: This is historical material, "frozen in time." The website is no longer updated and links to external websites and some internal pages will not work]

8. Bush On Jobs: The Worst Track Record On Record BY WSJ Staff, The Wall Street Journal, January 9, 2009. The Wall Street Journalhttp://blogs.wsj.com/economics/2009/01/09/bush-on-jobs-the-worst-track-record-on-record/

9. The 2001 and 2003 Bush Tax Cuts and Deficit Reduction - Thomas L. Hungerford Specialist in Public Finance, July 18, 2012. Congressional Research Service.   CRS Report for Congress. Congressional Research Service
 http://fas.org/sgp/crs/misc/R42020.pdf

10. H.R.4173 – Dodd Frank Wall Street Reform and Consumer Protection Act. 111th Congress (2009-2010),CONGRESS.GOV.
https://www.congress.gov/bill/111th-congress/house-bill/4173

11. MBA Chairman Robbins' Statement regarding the FHA Secure Initiative. Subject: President Bush, HUD, announce FHA Secure program and risk-based pricing initiative. August 31, 2007. Safeguard Properties
http://www.safeguardproperties.com/News/All_Client_
Alerts/2007/09/MBA_Chairman_Robbins_Statement_
regarding_the_FHA_Secure_Initiative.aspx

12. AllGov – Everything our Government Really Does – Occupational Safety and Health Administration (OSHA). AllGov
http://www.allgov.com/departments/department-of-labor/occupational-safety-and-health-administration-osha?agencyid=7167

13. OSHA Leaves Worker Safety in Hands of Industry, By Stephen Labaton, April 25, 2007. The New York Times. The New York Times

http://www.nytimes.com/2007/04/25/washington/25os
     ha.html?_r=0

14. Bush's Anti-union Record - By Joel Wendland 10
June, 2004 – Counter Currents .org. Counter Currents
.org.
http://www.countercurrents.org/us-
     wendland100604.htm

15. 2010. Legal Protection of Workers' Human Rights:
Regulatory Changes and Challenges in the United
States. Lance Compa Cornell University,
lac24@cornell.edu,
http://digitalcommons.ilr.cornell.edu/cgi/viewcontent.c
gi?article=1398&context=articles

16. Transcripts, Transcript Providers, CNN Breaking
News, Richard Clarke Testifies before 9/11
Commission, March 24, 2004. CNN.com
http://www.cnn.com/TRANSCRIPTS/0403/24/bn.00.ht
     ml

17. More Americans Now View Afghanistan War as a
Mistake: By Frank Newport, February 19, 2014,
GALLUP
http://www.gallup.com/poll/167471/americans-view-
     afghanistan-war-mistake.aspx

18. Ron Suskind, The Price of Loyalty: George W.
Bush, the White House and the Education of Paul
O'Neill

19. IRAQ - Ex-Weapons Inspector In Iraq Hoped
'There Would Not Be A War'. On the tenth
anniversary of the start of the Iraq war, Renee
Montagne talks to Hans Blix, the former chief U.N.

weapons inspector, who's mission in Iraq was ended by the invasion. NPR, March 19, 2013. Heard on Morning Edition. NPR http://www.npr.org/2013/03/19/174708587/u-n-weapons-inspector-looks-back-on-iraq-war

20. Top Bush officials push case against Saddam. WASHINGTON (CNN) -- September 8, 2002, Top officials in the Bush administration took to the Sunday television talk shows to argue the president's case that Iraqi President Saddam Hussein is a global threat and must go. CNN.com/insidepolitics CNN http://www.cnn.com/2002/ALLPOLITICS/09/08/iraq.debate/index.html?_s=PM:ALLPOLITICS

21. COSTS OF WAR, SUMMARY OF FINDINGS, Watson Institute for International and Public Affairs of the Brown University, Brown University http://watson.brown.edu/costsofwar/papers/summary

22. IMPACT, Research from Harvard Kennedy School, Counting the Costs of War, Harvard Kennedy School, John of Kennedy School of Government https://www.hks.harvard.edu/news-events/publications/impact-newsletter/archives/summer-2013/the-costs-of-the-iraq-and-afghanistan-wars

Chapter 2: Presidency of Barack Obama

1. The Clinton Camp Unbound, The Caucus, The Politics and Government blog of The New York Times. By Kate Phillips, January 8, 2008. The New York Times http://thecaucus.blogs.nytimes.com/2008/01/08/the-clinton-camp-unbound/?_r=0

2. Beck failed to ask Hagee about controversial statements, instead asked him if Obama might be the Antichrist. Research, March 5, 2008, Kirstin Ellison. MEDIAMATTERS For America http://mediamatters.org/research/2008/03/05/beck-failed-to-ask-hagee-about-controversial-st/142784

3. CNN Headline News' Glenn Beck on Obama: "[T]his guy really is a Marxist". Research, August 6, 2008, Morgan Weiland MEDIAMATTERS For America http://mediamatters.org/research/2008/08/06/cnn-headline-news-glenn-beck-on-obama-this-guy/144277

4. 'Meet the Press' transcript for October 19, 2008. Meet the Press on MEET THE PRESS. Former Secretary of State Gen. Colin Powell (Ret.) et al NBC News. http://www.nbcnews.com/id/27266223/ns/meet_the_press/t/meet-press-transcript-oct/#.VzEg1vkrLIU

5. Misperceptions persist about Obama's faith, but aren't so widespread. By Jennifer Agiesta CNN Polling Director, September 14, 2015. CNN Politics. http://www.cnn.com/2015/09/13/politics/barack-obama-religion-christian-misperceptions/index.html

6. H.R. 1 – American Recovery and Reinvestment Act of 2009 https://www.congress.gov/bill/111th-congress/house-bill/1

7. About the Recovery Act, About the Act, The WHITE HOUSE, The Recovery Act https://www.whitehouse.gov/recovery/about

8. Troubled Asset Relief Program (TARP) Information, Banking Information and Regulation, Board of Governors of the Federal Reserve System
https://www.federalreserve.gov/bankinforeg/tarpinfo.htm

9. Homeowner Affordability and Stability Plan Fact Sheet, Press Center, 2/18/2009. U.S. Department of the Treasury
https://www.treasury.gov/press-center/press-releases/Pages/20092181117388144.aspx

10. Help for Homeowners, Macon Phillips, February 18, 2009. Home- Blog. The White House
https://www.whitehouse.gov/blog/2009/02/18/help-homeowners

11. Bush announces $17.4 billion auto bailout. By Mike Allen and David Rogers, 12/19/08. Politico, POLITICO
http://www.politico.com/story/2008/12/bush-announces-174-billion-auto-bailout-016740

12. Obama on auto bailout, GM exodus: Detroit auto industry 'strong enough to stand on its own' By Michael Wayland, December 09, 2013. mlive.com
http://www.mlive.com/auto/index.ssf/2013/12/obama_on_auto_bailout_detroit.html

13. Remarks of President Barack Obama - Responsibly Ending the War in Iraq. Remarks of President Barack Obama - As Prepared for Delivery, Responsibly Ending the War in Iraq. Camp Lejeune, North Carolina. Friday, February 27, 2009 – The White House
https://www.whitehouse.gov/the-press-office/remarks-

president-barack-obama-ndash-responsibly-ending-war-iraq

14. Troops in Baghdad Cheer President Obama's Surprise Visit. By Jake Tapper, Sunlen Miller, Karen Travers, April 7, 2009 ABC News http://abcnews.go.com/Politics/story?id=7272544&page=1

15. Remarks by the President on Ending the War in Iraq. For Immediate Release, October 21, 2011. The White House, Office of the Press Secretary. The White House https://www.whitehouse.gov/the-press-office/2011/10/21/remarks-president-ending-war-iraq

16. Osama Bin Laden Dead, May 2, 2011 BY Macon Phillips,. Summary: President Obama addresses the Nation to announce that the United States has killed Osama bin Laden, the leader of al Queda. HOME – BLOG, The White House https://www.whitehouse.gov/blog/2011/05/02/osama-bin-laden-dead

17. H.R.4173 – Dodd-Frank Wall Street Reform and Consumer Protection Act 111th Congress (2009-2010) https://www.congress.gov/bill/111th-congress/house-bill/4173

18. HHS.Gov, Health Care. Read the Law. The Affordable Care Act was passed by Congress and then signed into law by the President on March 23, 2010. On June 28, 2012 the Supreme Court rendered a final decision to uphold the health care law

HHS.Gov
http://www.hhs.gov/healthcare/about-the-law/read-the-law/index.html

19. Health Insurance Coverage in the United States: 2014, Current Population Reports By Jessica C. Smith and Carla Medalia. Issued September 2015 Census.Gov
https://www.census.gov/content/dam/Census/library/publications/2015/demo/p60-253.pdf

20. Uninsured. The Henry J. Kaiser Family Foundation. The Henry J. Kaiser Family Foundation
http://kff.org/uninsured/

21. Health Care Coverage Under the Affordable Care Act – A Progress Report, The Common Wealth Fund
http://www.commonwealthfund.org/publications/in-the-literature/2014/jul/coverage-under-affordable-care-act-progress-report

22. Nations Approve Landmark Climate Accord in Paris, By Coral Davenport, December 12, 2015. The New York Times.
http://www.nytimes.com/2015/12/13/world/europe/climate-change-accord-paris.html?_r=0

23. Implementation Day, The Historic Deal that Will Prevent Iran from Acquiring a Nuclear Weapon. How the U.S. and the international community will block all of Iran's pathways to a nuclear weapon. Watch the President's remarks on the impact of U.S. leadership in Iran. The White House.
https://www.whitehouse.gov/issues/foreign-policy/iran-deal

Chapter 3: Chaos in the GOP

1. Book - Do Not Ask What Good We Do: Inside the U.S. House of Representatives by Robert Draper.

2. The Market Ticker
https://market-ticker.org/

3. The Market Ticker
https://tickerforum.org/

4. Tea Party February 1st? The Market Ticker – Commentary on The Capital Markets
https://market-ticker.org/akcs-www?singlepost=2137825

5. Mr. Graham Makohoniuk B – ZOOMinfo -
http://www.zoominfo.com/p/Graham-Makohoniuk/28384460

6. FedUpUSA – News & Information on the Economic Crisis, January 2009
http://www.fedupusa.org/OldSite.html#January09

7. Karl Denninger's Home on the Net
http://www.denninger.net/

8. Taking America back – By Edward Luce, October 30, 2010 – FT Magazine
http://www.ft.com/intl/cms/s/2/88143c46-e1e1-11df-b18d-00144feabdc0.html

9. Mary Rakovich's small protest against stimulus

erupted into 'tea party' movement - By David

Montgomery, Washington Post Staff Writer, May 29, 2010 – The Washington Post http://www.washingtonpost.com/wp-dyn/content/article/2010/05/28/AR2010052804673.html

10. History Commons, Context of 'February 16-17, 2009: Porkulus Rallies Protesting Obama Economic Policies Occur in Seattle, Denver; Rallies have 'Tea Party' Connections
http://www.historycommons.org/context.jsp?item=a02161709porkulusrallies

11. A Tax Day Tea Party cheat sheet: How it all started – By Michelle Malkin , April 15, 2009 – MICHELLE MALKIN -
http://michellemalkin.com/2009/04/15/a-tax-day-tea-party-cheat-sheet-how-it-all-started/

12. Tea Party Star Leads Movement On Her Own Terms, Martin Kaste, February 2, 2010 – NPR Special Series – the tea party in America -
http://www.npr.org/templates/story/story.php?storyId=123229743

13. Denver Stimulus Bill Protest 2009, Ballotpedia, The Encyclopedia of American Politics
https://ballotpedia.org/Denver_Stimulus_Bill_Protest_2009

14. Mesa Tax Protest 2009, Ballotpedia, The Encyclopedia of American Politics
https://ballotpedia.org/Mesa_Tax_Protest_2009

15. Rick Santelli: Tea party: February 19, 2009, Freedom Eden
http://freedomeden.blogspot.com/2009/02/rick-santelli-tea-party.html

16. Rick Santelli: Tea party Time, The New York Times: The Opinion Pages, Opinionator, by Eric Etheridge February 20, 2009
http://opinionator.blogs.nytimes.com/2009/02/20/rick-santelli-tea-party-time/?_r=0

17. Tea Party Protests, Birth of the national Tea Party movement.
https://en.wikipedia.org/wiki/Tea_Party_protests

18. Freedom Works, Source Watch, The Center for Media and Democracy
http://www.sourcewatch.org/index.php/FreedomWorks

19. Anatomy of the Tea party Movement: Americans for Prosperity, Produced by HuffPost, Eyes & Ears Citizen Journalism Unit, Alex Brant-Zawadzki and Dawn Teo, 3/18/2010, The Blog, Huffpost Politics, Huffington post
http://www.huffingtonpost.com/alex-brantzawadzki/anatomy-of-the-tea-party_b_380608.html

20. Tea Party Kingmaker Becomes Power Unto Himself, By Kate Zernike, Oct, 30, 2010, Politics, The New York Times
http://www.nytimes.com/2010/10/31/us/politics/31demint.html?_r=0

21. Obama Rips GOP Obstruction by Michele Richinick, 06/28/2014, MSNBC
http://www.msnbc.com/msnbc/obama-republicans-obstruction-economy

22. Jay Carney Says Obama Will 'Bypass Congress' in 2014, by Matt Sledge, 01/26/2014, Huffpost Politics, Huffington Post

http://www.huffingtonpost.com/2014/01/26/jay-carney-executive-acti_n_4669270.html

Chapter 4: Why Not Donald Trump

1. A Guide to Donald Trump's Business Career, International Business Degree Guide http://www.internationalbusinessguide.org/trump-business-career/

2. What the voters want – and don't want - in a presidential candidate by Carrie Dann, May 5, 2015, Meet the Press, NBC News http://www.nbcnews.com/meet-the-press/what-americans-want-dont-want-presidential-candidate-n354141

3. Citing Public Support, Trump Forms Exploratory Committee on Presidency by Robert D. McFadden, October 8, 1999. National Politics. New York Times on the Web http://partners.nytimes.com/library/politics/camp/100899wh-trump.html

4. Post Politics, Full text: Donald Trump announces a presidential bid by Washington Post Staff, June 16, 2015, The Washington Post https://www.washingtonpost.com/news/post-politics/wp/2015/06/16/full-text-donald-trump-announces-a-presidential-bid/

5. Ted Cruz's father- Caught with JFK Assassin by J.R. Taylor, April 20, 2016, National Enquirer http://www.nationalenquirer.com/celebrity/ted-cruz-scandal-father-jfk-assassination/

6. Fat Checker, "Donald Trump's false comments connecting Mexican Immigrants and crime" By Michelle Ye Hee Lee, July 8, 2015, Washington Post
https://www.washingtonpost.com/news/fact-checker/wp/2015/07/08/donald-trumps-false-comments-connecting-mexican-immigrants-and-crime/

7. Donald Trump says Mexican government 'forces many bad people into our country' - By Louis Jacobson on Thursday, July 9th, 2015, PolitiFact
http://www.politifact.com/truth-o-meter/statements/2015/jul/09/donald-trump/donald-trump-says-mexican-government-forces-many-b/

8. Immigration Reform that will make America great again, Trump, Make America great Again
https://www.donaldjtrump.com/images/uploads/Immigration-Reform-Trump.pdf

9. Let's say Trump wins. Would anyone design his border wall? By Kriston Capps, March 8, 2016. *From the Atlantic* CITILAB
http://www.citylab.com/work/2016/03/lets-say-trump-wins-would-anyone-design-his-border-wall/472065/

10. FactCheck: Trump's Immigration Plan, August 21, 2015. Philly.com, The Inquirer, Daily News
http://www.philly.com/philly/news/politics/FactCheck_Trumps_immigration_plan.html

11. Remarks as delivered by The Honorable James R. Clapper Director of National Intelligence. Senate Select Committee on Intelligence – IC's Worldwide Threat Assessment Opening Statement. Tuesday Feb 9, 2016 2:30 p.m. Hart Senate Office Building –

Washington DC
https://www.dni.gov/files/documents/2016-02-
09SSCI_open_threat_hearing_transcript.pdf

 12. Transcript: Donald Trump's National Security Speech
6/13/2016. Politoco.
http://www.politico.com/story/2016/06/transcript-donald-
trump-national-security-speech-224273

13. Read Donald Trump's Speech on Trade. TIME
STAFF, June 28,2016, TIME
http://time.com/4386335/donald-trump-trade-speech-
transcript/

14. Tax Reform that will make America great again.
TRUMP
https://www.economy.com/mark-zandi/documents/2016-
06-17-Trumps-Economic-Policies.pdf

15. The Macroeconomic Consequences of Mr. Trump's
Economic Policies, Moody's Analytics
https://www.economy.com/mark-zandi/documents/2016-
06-17-Trumps-Economic-Policies.pdf

16. Donald J. Trump's Foreign Policy Speech. April 27,
2016. TRUMP
https://www.donaldjtrump.com/press-releases/donald-j.-
trump-foreign-policy-speech

Chapter 5: Why Hillary

1. Pass It On. VALUES.COM
http://www.values.com/inspirational-quotes/7155-do-
all-the-good-you-can-by-all-the-means-you

2. The New World Mapper
http://www.worldmapper.org/display.php?selected=5

3. First Lady Biography: Hillary Clinton. National First Ladies Library.
http://www.firstladies.org/biographies/firstladies.aspx?biography=43

4. Hillary Clinton's Long, Committed Record Advocating for Women and Children, By DaisiesArePretty, Feb 18, 2016 Daily Kos
http://www.dailykos.com/story/2016/2/18/1487116/-Hillary-Clinton-s-Long-Committed-Record-Advocating-For-Women-and-Children

5. Our Mission, Children's Defense Fund
http://www.childrensdefense.org/about

6. Encyclopedia of Arkansas History and Culture. Arkansas Advocates for Children and Families
http://www.encyclopediaofarkansas.net/encyclopedia/entry-detail.aspx?entryID=2744

7. Children's Defense Fund. Encyclopedia.com
http://www.encyclopedia.com/topic/Childrens_Defense_Fund.aspx

8. Hillary Clinton. The White House Historical Association
https://www.whitehousehistory.org/bios/hillary-clinton

9. In Arkansas Hillary Clinton's Legacy Remains Potent, Scott Conroy, Senior Rolitical Reporter, 5/11/2015. The Huffington Post http://www.huffingtonpost.com/2015/05/11/hillary-clinton-arkansas_n_7258956.html

10. I was there when Hillary Clinton helped lead the bipartisan effort to create the Children's Health Insurance Program. David Nexon https://medium.com/@dnexon/i-was-there-when-hillary-clinton-helped-lead-the-bipartisan-effort-to-create-the-childrens-health-ac9920da0168

11. Hillary Clinton's Most Famous Feminist Speech Almost Never Happened. By Mattie Khan, Sep. 9, 2015 ELLE http://www.elle.com/culture/career-politics/news/a30328/hillary-clinton-beijing-speech/

12. What is Hillary's Greatest Accomplishment? POLITICOMAGAZINE http://www.politico.com/magazine/story/2015/09/carly-fiorina-debate-hillary-clintons-greatest-accomplishment-213157

13. The Lilly Ledbetter Fair Pay Act. Lilly Ledbetter http://lillyledbetter.com/

14. 1965 Johnson signs Voting Rights Act http://www.history.com/this-day-in-history/johnson-signs-voting-rights-act

15. Martin Luther King Jr. H/ History http://www.history.com/topics/black-history/martin-luther-king-jr

16. From Park Ridge to Washington: The youth minister who mentored Hillary Clinton. By Dan Merica, CNN, April 25, 2014. CNN Politics http://www.cnn.com/2014/04/25/politics/clinton-methodist-minister/

17. How 1968 Changed Hillary. Edward Mcclelland on April 8, 2008, SALON. Salon.com
http://www.salon.com/2008/04/08/hillary_1968/

18. Why I'm for Hillary Clinton. By Rodney Ellis, Feb. 18, 2016. TribTalk, a publication of the Texas Tribune
https://www.tribtalk.org/2016/02/18/why-im-for-hillary-clinton/

19. Transcript of Clinton's 'House Divided' Springfield speech. CHICAGO NEWS, 7/13/2016. Lynn Sweet. Chicago Sun Times
http://chicago.suntimes.com/news/hillary-clintons-house-divided-springfield-speech-transcript/

20. A transcript of Hillary Clinton's remarks on immigration reform Tuesday, May 5, 2015 • Rancho High School, Las Vegas
http://www.hagstromreport.com/assets/2015/2015_05 06_ClintonImmigrationRemarks.pdf

21. Transcript: President Obama's Democratic National Convention speech. July 27, 2016 By Los Angeles Staff. Los Angeles Times
http://www.latimes.com/politics/la-na-pol-obama-2016-convention-speech-transcript-20160727-snap-story.html

22. A Woman in Charge – Carl Bernstein
http://www.carlbernstein.com/awic.php

23. Senate Confirms Clinton as Secretary of State By

Kate Phillips, January 21, 2009, **The New York Times.**

http://thecaucus.blogs.nytimes.com/2009/01/21/senate-debates-clinton-confirmation/

24. U.S. Department of State – Diplomacy in Action.
http://www.state.gov/r/pa/ei/rls/dos/436.htm

25. Fact Sheet: The 2015 National Security Strategy.
The White House
https://www.whitehouse.gov/the-press-office/2015/02/06/fact-sheet-2015-national-security-strategy

26. Clinton won't promise Dem voter she wouldn't expand U.S. military involvement, by Gabby Morrongiello, 2/3/2016 Washington Examiner

http://www.washingtonexaminer.com/clinton-wont-promise-dem-voter-she-wouldnt-expand-u.s.-military-involvement/article/2582384

27. Yale University Commencement (June 11, 1962) John F. Kennedy. Transcript
http://millercenter.org/president/speeches/speech-3370

28. White House FBI files controversy. Wikipedia the Free Encyclopedia
https://en.wikipedia.org/wiki/White_House_FBI_files_controversy

29. Whitewater Controversy. Wikipedia the Free Encyclopedia
https://en.wikipedia.org/wiki/Whitewater_controversy

30. Starr: Vincent Foster's Death Was Suicide. July 15, 1997.

http://www.cnn.com/ALLPOLITICS/1997/07/15/starr.f
oster/

31. Suicide of Vince Foster. From Wikipedia, the free
encyclopedia
 https://en.wikipedia.org/wiki/Suicide_of_Vince_Foster

32. Benghazi Mission Attack Fast Facts. Updated 07-
20-2016 CNN Library
http://www.cnn.com/2013/09/10/world/benghazi-
consulate-attack-fast-facts/index.html

33. Seventh GOP Benghazi Investigation Finds No
Criminality Or Malfeasance – Eighth Inquiry Is Underway. By
Jon Ponder, 11-25-2014 Pensito Review.
http://www.pensitoreview.com/2014/11/25/seventh-gop-
benghazi-investigation-finds-no-criminality-or-malfeasance-
eighth-inquiry-is-underway/

34. Kevin McCarthy's comments about Benghazi should
trouble Republicans. By Chris Cillizza on September 30,
2015 The Washington Post
https://www.washingtonpost.com/news/the-
fix/wp/2015/09/30/kevin-mccarthys-comments-about-
benghazi-should-raise-a-red-flag-for-
republicans/?tid=a_inl

35. Richard Hanna and the GOP are handing Hillary
Clinton a Benghazi hearing win before it even starts.
by Chris Cillizza on October 15, 2015
https://www.washingtonpost.com/news/the-
fix/wp/2015/10/15/republicans-are-handing-hillary-
clinton-a-win-at-the-benghazi-hearing-before-it-even-
starts/

36. Benghazi hearing ends after extraordinary 11-hour grilling of Clinton. By contact reporters Evan Harper and David Lauter, October 22, 2015. Los Angeles Times
http://www.latimes.com/nation/politics/la-na-hillary-clinton-benghazi-testimony-20151022-story.html